Extract from map by Thomas Jefferys c.1751

Market Cross
Kirkby Lonsdale

Wilfrid M Harris

Kirkby Lonsdale market cross

THE LUNE VALLEY

AND

THE HOWGILL FELLS

W.R. Mitchell

PHILLIMORE

2009

Published by

PHILLIMORE & CO. LTD

Chichester, West Sussex, England

www.phillimore.co.uk

© W.R. Mitchell, 2009

ISBN 978-1-86077-550-5

Printed and bound in Great Britain

For

Rita and Phil Hudson

Contents

List of Illustrations

Acknowledgements

Richard Hall of the Cumbria Record Office, Kendal directed me to the illustrations in *The Annals of Kirkby Lonsdale* by Alexander Pearson, a book that was first published in 1930 and re-printed in recent times. Permission to use copies of the pictures was given by Canon Graham Bettridge, former Rector of Kirkby Lonsdale, and Mrs Audrey Phillips. Alan King advised on archaeology.

Phil Hudson, of Hudson History, based at Settle, was a prime source of information about the middle and lower reaches of the valley. Michael J. Hall's photographic compilation under the title *Old Kirkby Lonsdale and the Rainbow Parish* was valuable both pictorially and factually. Support was extended by the headmaster of Sedbergh School and Katy Iliffe, the archivist, and by Dr P. McLaughlin (headmaster of Casterton School) and Dorothy Vernon, a member of his staff who has the care of the school archives.

Inquiries into the Brontë associations with the Leck and Cowan Bridge areas were aided by a family connection with the famous family – a great great grandfather of mine having been a personal friend of Patrick Brontë – and by Jane Ewbank's biography of William Carus Wilson, who established the Clergy Daughters' School attended by the Brontë girls. Dr Florence A.M. Wellburn imparted knowledge of Leck Church when I led a party of local historians to the area.

Alfred Wainwright, a personal friend, had already excited my interest in the Howgill Fells. In 1972 he penned a guide book to the area in his inimitable hand-written, hand-drawn style. We occasionally discussed the landscape quality of the Howgills, of which he wote, lyrically, 'They are sleek and smooth … velvet curtains in sunlight, like silken drapes at sunset.' Edward Jeffrey, an artist living at Ravenstonedale, provided me with sketches made from my photographs, his work investing people, places and things with a special character.

Jonty Wilson, born in 1893, the last decade of Queen Victoria's reign, was for over sixty years a blacksmith at Kirkby Lonsdale. His passion for local history and extraordinary memory for people, places and things were often at my disposal. His daughters, Audrey and Hilda, gave unstinting help during my research. Hand-knitting was important industrially, especially in the upper dale. John Austin provided me with additional information about local angling. Freda Trott (née Douglas Kay), who died in 2008, had been a valued contributor on local topics to *The Dalesman* during my editorship and was generous in allowing the use of photographs and taped interviews with a host of interesting people. With Bob Swallow and Colin Pomfret as fellow walkers, I explored the area under review in the best possible way – on foot.

Illustrations from the following sources are cordially acknowledged: Freda Trott, 4, 5; David Binns, 8, 13, 141, 143; *The Annals of Kirkby Lonsdale*, 14, 15, 38, 49, 50, 51, 52, 68; Lancaster Maritime Museum, 25, 26, 27, 28; Collection of Dr A.J. White, 16, 17, 18; Lancaster Library, 19; Lancaster and Morecambe Newspapers Picture Library, 21, 22, 23, 24; Society of Friends: 43; Sedbergh and District History Society, 95, 96; Geoffrey N. Wright, *per* Yorkshire Dales Society, 74; Celia King, 100; Godfrey Wilson, 101; Derek Cross collection, via David Joy, 110, 112, 113, 116, 117, 118; Gordon Biddle, 114, 115; David Hoyle, 121; Sedbergh School, 127, 128, 129, 130; Casterton School, 133, 134, 135. All other photographs are by the author. Drawings by the late Edward Jeffrey were specially drawn from the author's photographs.

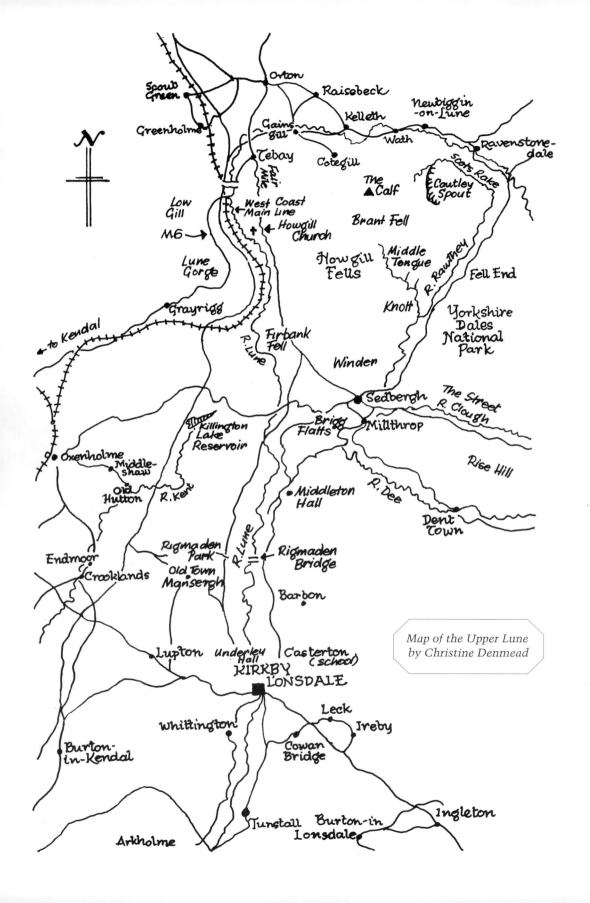

Map of the Upper Lune
by Christine Denmead

Chapter 1

River Lune

Water that feeds the infant Lune flows from Green Bell, an austere hill on the northern flank of the Howgill Fells. The name Lune is first used when two becks, Sandwath and Weasdale, blend their waters at Wath, the name signifying a ford, in the parish of Ravenstonedale. The first village is aptly named Newbiggin-on-Lune. From its source, the Lune flows for 44 miles to an estuary and has its official termination on an imaginary line between Heysham and Fleetwood.

In glacial times, the Lune's watershed took in what are now the headwaters of the Eden as well as the northern part of the Howgills. Surely no English river can have had more names bestowed on it. The oldest, possibly pre-Celtic, are 'Loun', 'Loin', 'Loyn' and 'Lon'. From the Lune is derived the place-name Lancaster, and therefore Lancashire. The river is said to have been in the mind of J.R.R. Tolkein when, devising Middle Earth, he named his imaginary river Lhun. The names Lune Valley and Vale of Lune became popular, having a dash of romance. The valley has changes of name en route: Lunesdale in its upper reaches, and Lonsdale from Tebay, where it takes a southwards course through a steep-sided reach grandly known as the Lune Gorge, extending between Lune's Bridge at Tebay, and Crook o' Lune Bridge near Beckfoot.

The river has innumerable tributaries, each of which is fed by moorland becks. Not far from its source, Cautley Spout descends the steep eastern flank of the Howgill Fells in a series of gigantic leaps totalling 700 feet. The watercourse then joins a trio of lively rivers, Rawthey, Clough and Dee, that blend their waters with the Lune in the vicinity of Sedbergh. Notable inflows much further down the Lune are Barbon and Leck Becks and the Rivers Greta, Wenning and Condor. Generally, apart from the floodplains of Tebay and the lower valley, the Lune's bed is deep enough to ensure the river keeps within

1

1 *House at Wath near Newbiggin-on-Lune.*

its banks, although one Martinmas a torrent of rain fell on to already soaked ground around the headwaters in Ravenstonedale and surged down the valley at such a height that old stone bridges were only just able to cope and a man who stood on Crook o'Lune Bridge, near Lancaster, claimed he felt it vibrate beneath him, 'as if I was standing on a riddling machine'. In the spring of 1927, when the Lune froze to a depth of about two feet six inches, it was a skater's paradise.

The Lune flows by Orton, north of Tebay, a village backed by limestone country and known to the many who have undertaken Alfred Wainwright's Coast to Coast Walk. In the valley of the Lyvennet, north of Orton, is a scattering of 'thunderstones' composed of Shap pink granite. Boulders plucked by glacial ice from an area scarcely a square mile in size were dropped at random over a vast area. Softer rocks were ground to mush by the Pleistocene ice but the pink granite, smoothed by the glacier, remained in lumps averaging about six tons. A specimen of thirteen tons weight, transported from this area to Heaton Park, Manchester, was the centrepiece for a decorative area created for the recent visit of a Pope. Orton was one of five market towns in Westmorland and retains its village stocks – as a curiosity. The market charter, awarded by Henry II and ratified in the reign of Edward I, was confirmed in Cromwellian times. The church at Orton had been appropriated to Conishead Priory about 1150 and it was the Priory who

THE HIGH CHAPEL

RAVENSTONEDALE

St. OSWALD'S CHURCH

TARN HOUSE 1664

BASE OF SAXON CROSS

c. jeffrey

2 *Ravenstonedale, near the source of the Lune (by local artist Edward Jeffrey).*

appointed the vicar up to the Dissolution in 1536. Then the Crown took over the advowson, which in 1612 was owned by two London speculators. The Vicar of Orton negotiated the purchase in trust, and thereafter the landowners of Orton appointed the vicar by ballot. Nicholas Close, the architect of King's College, Cambridge was born here. He became Bishop of Carlisle in 1450 and died as Bishop of Lichfield in 1452. A royal coat of arms of 1695 implies the church was loyal to King William III. The medieval parish chest is a curiosity. Bound in iron, and with three locks, it defies further investigation.

In the mid-1880s, when Bulmer published his review of Westmorland, Orton had just acquired a new and spacious market house. Three fairs took place in the broad streets each year and the township had two blacksmiths,

PETTY HALL

GB 1604 MB

Orton

BELLS IN
THE NAVE OF
THE CHURCH

3   *Orton village, upper Lunesdale (by Edward Jeffrey).*

three makers of footwear, five drapers, two dressmakers, seven grocers and shopkeepers, three inns, an ironmonger, four joiners and wheelwrights, two masons, three slaters, three tailors, and drapers.

The upper valley of the Lune, geologically and administratively, is split between the Lake District and the Yorkshire Dales. The geological split, known as the Dent Fault, separates the Silurian rocks of the Lakes and the Carboniferous rocks of the Dales. A section of the fault-line, exposed by the River Clough, a tributary of the Lune, was designated the Sedgwick Geological Trail in 1985, the bicentenary year of the birth of Adam Sedgwick (1785-1873). It was this distinguished geologist, a native of Dent, who first described the fault-line. Sedgwick, who became Woodwardian Professor of Geology at Cambridge, and is regarded as the 'father' of geology, made the first systematic study of the Lakeland rocks. A close friend of William Wordsworth, he contributed five letters on geology to the poet's *Guide to the Lakes*. Sedgwick's paper in the *Transactions* of the Geological Society in 1835 contains his description of the stages by which he unravelled the Dent Fault. A contrast in the ancient landscape is the large expanse of water at Killington, adjacent to the M6 service station to the north of the Lune Gap. It is a reservoir formed by the damming of the Pizzey Beck and was originally intended to feed the Lancaster Canal.

4 *The mill at Howgill, which gave its name to the Howgill Fells.*

The motorway, in its course through the Gap, shares the valley with the old road – at a higher level – and the main Glasgow railway. The Howgill Fells, to the east, shout to be noticed. On their lower flanks are traces of a former Roman road, now known as the Fair Mile. The name Howgill is that of a secluded little community situated to the west of the fells and is derived from 'howe', or hill, and 'gill', a narrow, water-carved valley. The significance of the name was evident when, following torrential rain, an estimated 2,000 tons of rubble was washed from the fells and demolished part of the wall of the church dating from 1838. The drive and vision of a curate, the Rev. Isaac Green, brought Howgill Church into existence. The village throve when its principal workplace was a woollen mill.

The Howgill Fells might give the impression they can be taken in at a glance, but those who walk steadily uphill to the summit of the Calf, the high spot, see water-carved recesses known as gills. Carlin Gill (west) has a spectacular hidden waterfall. Prior to the boundary revision of 1974, this gill was on the boundary between the West Riding of Yorkshire and Westmorland. Cautley Spout, another local spectacle, is approached on a bridge and path beginning near an isolated roadside inn, *The Cross Keys*, which stands beside the road to Kirkby Stephen and is owned by the National Trust. The earliest records of *The Cross Keys* relate to 1619, when it was the home of one Thomas Bland. The property was extended in each century until it attained its present size. In the early part of the 18th century, it was a small farmhouse known as High Haygarth. The initials and date that are carved into the stone above the front door refer to John and Agnes Howgill, who owned the place in 1732. As *The Cross Keys* it throve until the inn

5 *Howgill Mill, near Sedbergh.*

6   The Cross Keys, *Cautley, photographed in strong morning sunshine.*

status was assumed. Sold to Mrs Edith Bunney, who had the liquor licence removed, the property was then willed to the National Trust in memory of Edith's sister, Miss Mary Blanche Hewetson.

A serious climber, glancing at the Howgill Fells, might concluded there is nothing to interest him or her. Yet, as A.H. Griffin once observed, 'For the walker or the skier, it is superb country, with clean, lonely hills, inhabited by sheep, buzzards and larks; an occasional tumbling beck; plenty of fresh air all round and views full of blue sky and sunshine ... Potentially, the Howgill Fells are the best skiing country in the north of England; they are smooth and rounded, grow little or no heather, carry no stone walls and sport few crags or screes, while the fell grass needs only a slight covering of snow to be negotiable.' Alfred Wainwright, in his guide to the Howgill Fells, was intrigued by the

7   *Walking towards the Calf, Howgill Fells.*

close affinity of place-names with those of the Lake District. Besides the basic names for geographical features, in and about the Howgills 'is another Langdale, another Borrowdale, another Bowderdale, another Grisedale. And another Harter Fell … '

8 *The raven, gruff-voiced bird of the high crags.*

Cumbria claims the fells lying to the south of the Calf and also Baugh Fell, fell pony country. Fell ponies are not fussed over, many dropping their foals in the wild. A pony that has been broken might be usefully employed by a shepherd on the fells: one was harnessed to a sled that had been hastily made so hay could be moved to the outlying stock.

A traveller who leaves the M6 for the Lowgill road to Sedbergh has the River Lune in view from time to time. In prominent view initially is a disused railway viaduct, a reminder of the old Ingleton-Tebay branch line. The Lowgill railway viaduct, which took shape in 1860, has 11 arches and a height of 100 feet. A motorist driving under one of the arches passes what used to be the Davy Bank watermill and follows a narrow road to where the Lune is spanned by a narrow 16th-century bridge. This part of the Lune valley is noted for narrow roads flanked by tall hedges.

9 *Walkers approaching Cautley Spout.*

10 *Stone marking the boundary between the West Riding and Westmorland, Howgill Fells in the background.*

Sedbergh's river is the Rawthey, a prime tributary of the Lune. Administratively, Sedbergh was transferred in the boundary changes of 1974 to the new county of Cumbria, yet the town continues to be a part of the Yorkshire Dales National Park. Among the dales that converge on Sedbergh are Dentdale and Garsdale. The main dale assumes the U-shape of the typical glacier-hewn valley, a characteristic it will retain for most of the remaining course. Breezes wafted updale give the valley a milder if wetter climate than the area to the east. On the floodplain, the course of the river in historic times has lacked stability. Thomas Grey, in a letter to Thomas Warton of 18 October 1769, published in 1775, was referring to the lower reaches when he wrote of the Lune as 'winding in a deep valley, its hanging banks clothed with fine woods, through which you catch long reaches of the water, as the road winds about at considerable height above it'.

Limestone is a feature of the valley. On and around Casterton Fell, the limestone is honeycombed with potholes and caves. Excursions to Leck Fell during 1929 led members of the Gritstone Club into Peterson Pot and the quaintly named Pippikin and Nippikin Pots. Lancaster Hole, a pothole on a grand scale, festooned with stalactites, was discovered by accident when a man sat down for a rest on a calm day and saw grass being disturbed by a draught emanating from beneath his feet. Miles of passages were painstakingly

11 *Bridge near Davy Bank Mill across the River Lune. The miller had to reduce the width of his lorry in order to use it.*

12 *The River Lune at Lowgill, with a means of crossing dryshod.*

explored. Limestone has been exposed and weathered into 'pavement' form at Hutton Roof. At Kirkby Lonsdale the river cuts through the eastern arm of a major deposit of limestone extending from Kendal to Carnforth and is spanned by a medieval bridge with satanic associations. The Devil's Bridge was on the main Keighley-Kendal road until a new bridge was constructed, a short distance downriver, in 1932.

At Cowan Bridge a tributary of the Lune gains strength. A row of cottages here was once a school and was made notorious through the writings of Charlotte Brontë. Patrick, the father of Charlotte, was curate at Haworth and a widower. He decided in 1824 that his daughters, Marie, Elizabeth, Charlotte and Emily, would become boarders at a Clergy Daughters' School which Carus Wilson had established, but an attack of low fever and relatively poor conditions led to the deaths of Maria and Elizabeth. When, in 1846, Charlotte penned her novel *Jane Eyre*, the school became 'Lowood'. The grim conditions here were somewhat unfairly described.

13 *The dipper, a bird of fast-flowing clear water.*

Lower down the valley the hills are relatively low and well spaced. There are tantalising glimpses of Ingleborough, one of the Pennine flat-tops. The Lune between Arkholme and Melling is in a floodplain and there is much evidence

14   *River Lune and Devil's Bridge in 1849.*

of changes in its course. The single street of Arkholme, north of the river, leads down to a fording place. Spacious and green, the plain has long been a wintering ground for wild geese, especially Icelandic greylags.

At Hornby, the Lancaster-bound roadway becomes as wide and straight as an arrow-flight before taking a sharp right turn towards the city. In the background is a range of low rounded hills occupying the eastern fringe of Bowland. Enough remains at Hornby from olden times to give the village a venerable appearance. A lofty gateway leads to Hornby Castle, which is set on an isolated hill-top close to the River Wenning. A private house, rarely open to the public and best viewed from a bank of the Wenning, the dramatic building looks ancient but is mainly of 19th-century work. All that is left of a medieval castle is the great tower dating from the early years of the 16th century. Dr A.J. White, in a history and guide to the castle, observes that its position recalls chateaux of the Loire and the Rhineland. A traveller moving updale in autumn is arrested by the redness of the creeper on the walls.

Hornby Institute, designed by Austin and Paley of Lancaster and paid for by Colonel Foster, lord of the manor, in honour of his son's coming of age, was completed in 1916. Originally used mainly by men, it has been extended

15 *North side of the Devil's Bridge, engraved by William Green.*

and restored over the years and now serves the community as a resource centre, efficiently run by the Hornby Village Trust.

Caton, a stylish village, grew around two local becks, one of them draining Littledale. Caton and other local villages are now associated with the Forest of Bowland Area of Outstanding Natural Beauty. At the Crook o' Lune, near Caton, the river's even course through deposits of glacial drift bends sharply on reaching a rocky area. The name of the stretch refers to the river's shape, which is that of a shepherd's crook. Long respected as a beauty spot and a place at which to linger, the Crook o' Lune was romanticised through the art of J.M.W. Turner and the writing of William Wordsworth.

Halton's importance was established before the Norman Conquest, when Earl Tostig, the brother of King Harold, held the manor. In the 12th century the castle was abandoned and its importance assumed by Lancaster ('Lune Castle'). The Lune Aqueduct, 664 feet long, was designed by John Rennie. A notable engineer, Alexander Stephens, was involved in its construction.

THE EAST VIEW OF HORNBY CASTLE, NEAR LANCASTER.

THIS Castle is beautifully situated on a Hill, round the foot of which runs the river Wenning. It was founded by Nicholas de Mont Begon and after belonged to the Noble Families of the Harringtons & Stanleys Barons de Mont Aquila or Monteagle, descended from Thomas Stanley Earl of Derby: William Stanley the third & last Baron of Monteagle of that Name, left only a Daughter named Elizabeth, who married Edwd Parker Lord Morley, and had a Son William, who was restored by K. James 1st to the Barony of Monteagle.

16 *Hornby Castle, S & N Buck 1727*

17 *Hornby Castle, Pickering 1829*

18 *Hornby Castle, Banks & Son c.1850*

19 *View of Lancaster above the tidal Lune in 1780.*

20 *The impressive gateway of Lancaster Castle.*

21 *Glasson Dock from the air. The dock dates from 1787, and was constructed when navigation to Lancaster became difficult because of silting. It was connected to a branch of the Lancaster Canal.*

The Lune becomes tidal below Skerton Weir at Lancaster, where a sense of permanency is imparted by castle and church in prominent view on a hill. The merchants of Georgian Lancaster drew large profits from shipping on the estuary of the Lune. Early in the 18th century this was the fourth busiest port in the land. Later that century, in what would later be called 'the Golden Age of Lancaster shipping', merchants were enriched through trading with the West Indies. Goods discharged on the Lune at St George's Quay included sugar, rum, tobacco and cotton.

Charles Dickens, who visited Lancaster in 1857, wrote of 'staid old houses richly fitted with old Honduras mahogany ... ' He touched briefly on the subject of slaves, which at Lancaster was low in number compared with those being landed at Liverpool further along the Lancashire coastline. Quakers were among those who pioneered the shipping trade at Lancaster and many fine buildings of the Georgian period indicate that when merchants were not making money they enhanced their home acres with stylish buildings. At a time when Quakers were being persecuted, some escaped from the torment by sailing from Lancaster on ships bound for what would hopefully be better prospects in the New World.

The decline of Lancaster as a port was a consequence of the shallow state of the river and the existence of a rock bar close to the Quay. The situation led in 1787 to the creation by the Lancaster Port Commissioners, on the southern bank of the Lune, of Glasson Dock, the gates to which were closed at high tide to keep boats within afloat. The Dock was linked with the Lancaster Canal. Twenty-five merchantmen could be accommodated at Glasson Dock, which prospered at the expense of Sunderland Point. On this vacated shoreline stands the *Golden Ball*, a popular riverside inn that is better known as 'Snatchems', supposedly because naval press gangs found unwilling recruits here as well as at local farms and villages. The village of Overton, on a modest hill, depends both on the land and the Lune. It

22   A tidal reach of the Lune viewed from a reinforced bank. Lancaster was a city that drew much of its wealth from shipping.

23 *Sunderland is approached from the village of Overton by a narrow road one and a half miles in length. The road is overswept by a high tide.*

24 *Sunderland, also known as Sunderland Point, was developed in the early 18th century to serve as an outport for Lancaster by a Quaker named Robert Lawson.*

was noted for a type of fishing boat known as a 'nobby'. Salmon were caught Norse-style by men wading in the current with wide-sweeping haaf-nets. It was said, 'He that will fish for a Lancashire man, at any time or tide, Must baite his hooke with a good Eg-pie or an apple with a red side.'

Across the Lune, the Rector of Cockerham, a village some eight miles south of Lancaster, received an unusual tithe. He was permitted to claim salmon caught in the Lune channel baulk on the early morning tide every fortnight in the season. Also available

25 *River pilots on the Lune, 1900.*

to him were any fish left in the trap at the first tide after each new moon and full moon, this being known as 'the Vicar's tide'. Mid way through the 20th century, Herbert C. Collins was told about it by Richard Raby, the rector who, twice a day, from April to August, and at the age of 84 cycled down Thornham Moss to attend the baulk. He did the same in winter to make necessary repairs.

The road connecting Overton with Sunderland Point is usable by wheeled traffic on a part-time basis, a flow tide sweeping over it. This was one reason why Glasson Dock succeeded Sunderland Point for shipping, another being Sunderland's exposure to south-westerly gales. The shipping facilities nearest the mouth of the River Lune had enjoyed glorious moments

26 *Watchtower at Sunderland Point.*

27 *'Cotton tree' at Sunderland Point.*

ever since Robert Lawson, a Quaker merchant, built ships and warehouses here. Lawson traded with the West Indies, importing rum, tobacco, cotton wool (the kapok variety) and slaves. One of these, Samboo, temporarily left at Sunderland Point in 1736 by a sea captain who had business in Lancaster, pined to death in the belief his master had deserted him. The Lune estuary lost its importance in the 19th century when Liverpool became the main port on the Lancashire coast.

28 *River Lune near Sunderland Point, 1900.*

Chapter 2

Early Days

Human activity in and about the Lune is first associated with the free-draining limestone areas and along ridge routes used by travellers. William Rollinson, reviewing the history of man in the Lake District, believed that in pre-Roman times the native Cumbrians were essentially a hybrid group having characteristics that belonged to the Neolithic as well as the Bronze Age. In the mild climate of the Bronze Age, stone circles were erected on Casterton and Barbon Fells. Casterton's embanked circle is situated a mile east of the present village, 19 stones forming an almost perfect circle 20 yards in diameter. Several holes in the flat inner area of the circle may be the result of opportunist digging. The discovery by one John Tatham of several objects at the 'Druid's Temple', almost certainly Casterton, was reported in the *Westmorland Advertiser and Kendal Chronicle* for 29 March 1828. Tatham unearthed a bronze spearhead, a flint arrowhead and an 'antique drinking vessel'. An insight into life in the Bronze Age occurred when potholers ventured into water-filled passages eight miles north-east of Sedbergh and located a burial chamber that became popularly known as Wolf Hole. Along with the bones of wolf were human remains assessed at 3,500 years old. Human footprints were impressed on part of the cave floor. A Bronze-Age woman interred in the Wolf Hole was estimated to have been 48 years of age at death. Also found were the bones of a middle-aged man and a 15-year-old child.

In Celtic times lower fellsides were being cleared of trees. Traces of circular, thatched homes have been found at Barbon, Middleton and Leck. The skull of a horse, an animal held sacred

29 *Early man.*

in Celtic times, was a feature in a burial mound on the Common at Crosby Ravensworth. Of the eight British settlements in the parish of Crosby Ravensworth, those known as Ewe Close and Burwens were regarded as being especially important. Ewe Close was the home of around sixty people and lay on a well-drained fell-top in limestone country, clear of the primeval forest. The site, at an elevation of 850 feet, consists of a square-shaped walled village which was rather more than an acre in extent. There was a plethora of irregular enclosures, which were stone-walled, and the foundations of a number of huts were traced. In a central position was a circular hut with an impressive diameter of 50 feet which was paved with stone. A primitive form of fireplace was found in a smaller hut. At Burwens, across the valley, were mainly single-family farmsteads supporting an estimated population of some 200 people. Their sheep and cattle grazed the hills. Rotary querns were used for processing grain.

On the eve of the Roman invasion of Britain, in AD 43, Lunesdale was part of the vast tribal realm of the Brigantes, a stern and warlike people. Following the Roman defeat of the Brigantes, whether in one large battle or by three or four years of raids and skirmishes, the Pennine folk were controlled by a military presence based in small forts. The Brigantes, in turn, had hill-forts, and these defended areas existed on Warton Crag, near Carnforth, and on Castlesteads, at Natland, south-west of Kendal. The Romans quickly assessed the importance of a hill at what became Lancaster. It overlooked a broad reach of the river and its most convenient fords. Father West, the historian of Furness, claimed that the Romans' hatred and fear of the Scots began when Julius Agricola 'secured the Lune fords by a fort on the hill against the Caledonians, the unconquered enemies and greatest plague of the Romans in Britain'.

The first Roman buildings were of wood, with flanking ditches, the displaced earth providing material for ramparts. Eventually stone structures rested on foundations of blue clay, which, being impervious to water, was an ideal form of damp course. A strong force would have been maintained as this was a military district. Kilns at a pottery at nearby Quernmore Park yielded coarse ware, tiles and bricks. After Roman influence waned, the fort on the hill was callously robbed of stone and larger parts of the old settlement were eventually obscured by new buildings. What remained in use was a Roman road, extending from Lancaster on roughly the same line as the present highway to Over Burrow, near Kirkby Lonsdale. Two Roman milestones were found about a mile and a half from Ashton Hall at Lancaster. A milestone to the Emperor Hadrian was recovered from Arkle Beck at Caton.

The Romans established taxation and took over and enlarged the lead-mining and other industries. Large quantities of cereals were needed to feed the troops, who probably numbered about 300,000, as well as the followers, cavalry and draught animals. The small native British farmsteads around the Howgills and Kirkby Lonsdale increased production to be able to cater for the invaders. Roman soldiers were also keen to use the 'birrus Britannicus', a woollen cape with a hood that was ideal for cold winter patrols. They livened up its appearance with small bronze brooches, some of which were enamelled. The presence of a disciplined military force in the Lune Valley, based on three forts, ensured a long period of peace.

A Roman fort at Burrow, updale from Lancaster, was in existence for three and a half centuries. Sited at the point where Leck Beck flowed into the Lune, about two miles south of Kirkby Lonsdale, its remains were described by William Camden in 1610. Over-Burrow was then 'a very small village of husbandmen;

30 *Impression of a potholer. The Wolf Cave near Cautley contained bones of early humans.*

which, as the inhabitants enformed mee, had been sometimes a great City, and took up all those large fields between *Lacca* and *Lone*, and after it had suffered all miseries that follow famine, was driven to composition through extremity. This tradition they received from their ancestours, delivered as it were from hand to hand unto them. And in very truth by divers and sundry monuments exceeding ancient, by engraven stones, pavements of square checker worke, peeces of Roman coine, and by

31 *Hard, brittle coal, such as was mined on Casterton Fell.*

this new name *Burrow*, which with us signifieth a *Burgh*, that place should seeme to bee of great antiquity.'

Burrow Hall, rebuilt on the instructions and with the monies of Thomas Fenwick in 1740, covers a large part of the fort. Indeed, work on the hall led to the fort's rediscovery. The private drive leading to the house was originally an approach to that fort. In nearby Tunstall church is preserved part of a Roman altar. A votive stone, it refers to Asclepius, Greek god of medicine, and Hygieia,

32 *The Big Stone, traditional meeting place of Yorkshire, Lancashire and Westmorland.*

the goddess of health. Tom Garlick, in his study of Romans in the Lake Counties, mentions the discovery of four Roman inscriptions: an altar to the god Contrebis by a civilian, a family tombstone from Tunstall, an altar to Apollo from Kirkby Lonsdale, and a dedication by a Roman doctor to the patron deity of the medical profession.

The Roman road was indicated at Middleton, beyond Kirkby Lonsdale, by a milestone described by Professor R.G. Collingwood as 'the best Roman milestone in the country'. Cylindrical, it reaches a height of five feet six inches. The front is inscribed M P LIII – fifty-three miles – the distance from Carlisle. Diamond patterned markings on the back are thought to have been caused when the stone, lying just under the surface of the ground, was repeatedly scraped during ploughing. When it was unearthed by a ploughman in 1836, Squire William Moore had it shifted to where it now stands, some 200 yards from its original position.

A fort at Low Borrow Bridge, in the Lune Gorge south of Tebay, was much larger than the extent of the present level enclosure implies. It stood on a spur of land, a glacial moraine, where the Lune Gorge is joined by a small valley called Borrowdale. It is supposed that the fort housed an infantry battalion of 500 men, their main task being to keep open the vital route through the Lune Gorge. A reference in 1777 to this strangely isolated fort describes it as a castle. It was the first Roman fort to be dug by the Cumberland and Westmorland Archaeological Society. Until the early 19th century, its walls were standing to a considerable height, but some of the masonry was then used in the construction of farm buildings. Defensive ditches surrounded the fort and it is assumed that any visitor would first enter a civil settlement.

Boys of Sedbergh School, under an enlightened history teacher, found traces of the Roman road south of Tebay. John Anstee, an archaeologist who became curator of the Museum of Lakeland Life and Industry at Kendal, had read a little about the site but did not work there until 1973. The Wilson family, owners of the land, encountered the remains of old stone buildings while digging out the footings for a new barn and John was asked by the County Council to keep a watching brief. Scrappy and minor excavations over the previous hundred years had yielded little information about the fort, the exception being a report published by Hildyard and Gillam in 1951. With the permission of the Wilsons, Anstee investigated old stonework and realised that here was one of the stokeholes of a Roman bathhouse, traces of which were originally located by antiquarians in 1885. Like most Roman bathhouses, it stood outside the fort and was at least sixty feet in length. The site of the fort being relatively flat, it became known as Fair Field, after an annual fair which lasted until about a century ago. Livestock had been bought and sold and sports included Cumbrian-style wrestling.

No worthwhile Roman inscriptions have been found, although about ninety years ago a tombstone to a cavalry trooper was unearthed a mile to the south by two roadmen digging a culvert. Judging from the description made at the time it was a typical tombstone, showing a horseman, his legs dangling, apparently plunging a lance into the body of a Briton who lay beneath the horse's hooves. The Roman road, some twenty feet wide, ran along the western flanks of the Howgill Fells, bridges being formed of heavy timbers set on stone piers and abutments. The road passed through Crosby Ravensworth to Brougham, where it joined a road that crossed Stainmore to Brougham and continued to Carlisle.

For almost four centuries, the Roman war machine took control of a small indigenous population in poor, hilly country. In the seventh century Angles from what is now northern Germany established *tuns* (or farmsteads), and the suffix 'ton' is incorporated in the names Casterton, Middleton and Killington. H.A.L. Rice in 1983 summed up the Anglo-Saxons as 'mighty

33 *View across the Lune Gorge of part of the Howgill range of fells.*

men of the woodlands'. They cleared tracts of forest 'in order to build their "hut-tons", their "bar(n)tons", their middletons and, after they had become Christians, their "priest-tons".' The last of these probably alludes to the missionary who brought the faith. Anglian estates were given to Earl Tostig who, from a manor at Halton, ruled the Lune Valley as far north as Sedbergh.

Two centuries later, Danes were farming the lowlands, mainly in the east although the place-name suffix *-by* appears in Kirkby Lonsdale. In the tenth century, Norsefolk spread out from Galloway or from the Isle of Man, extending their pastoral activities across the virtually empty fells, where they might build longhouses on sites handy to springs or becks, graze livestock and tend their pigs. The suffix *-thwaite* relates to their clearings, *-garth* to an enclosure and *-wath* to a ford. Summertime grazings for livestock were known as *saeters*. Wild boar and deer were among the food items they hunted.

With the coming of the Normans, baronies were created, castles built and, with handsome grants from new landowners, the monastic system flourished, providing stability and order for well over four centuries. Shortly after the Norman Conquest, Roger de Poictou, with a substantial grant of land made by William I, fortified the hill at Lancaster, then occupied much of his time pushing the Scots further north, thereby establishing an Anglo-Scottish border.

Roger's tenure was short because, unwisely, he supported his brother, Robert of Belleme, against the Crown. He and his family were expelled in 1102 and the King claimed his estates. Richard I, preoccupied by affairs in the Holy Land, handed over the Honour of Lancaster to John, Earl of Mortain. During the reign of Edward III, what was now the dukedom was acquired through marriage by John o'Gaunt, the fourth son of the King, who began work on what would become the imposing gateway of Lancaster Castle in a spirit of ostentation. Northwards, a mound at Kirkby Lonsdale was subsequently named Cockpit Hill, doubtless a reference to the old sport of cock-fighting. Mounds are to be seen at Castlehaw (Sedbergh) and Castle Howe (Tebay), the latter occupying an area of about one and three quarter acres. In Domesday

34 *Memorial fountain to Sedgwick, the geologist, at Dent.*

35 *Dr T.D. Whitaker, historian of Craven.*

Book of 1086 AD, what is now the village of Barbon was *Berebrune*, signifying a farm standing beside a spring.

At the other end of the building scale were the many fortresses of the motte-and-bailey type. The motte was an artificial mound, shaped like an upturned pudding dish, on which stood a tower used by the lord and his family as a refuge in times of travail. An impressively large ditch separated the motte from the bailey, where – behind earthen bank and timber palisade – stood stables and storehouses and a timber hall. The bridge that spanned the ditch was of a type that might easily be jettisoned if the motte were to become a refuge from attackers. Whittington church, in the valley below Kirkby Lonsdale, occupies the site of a motte and bailey castle. The dedication is to St Michael the Archangel, who was often called upon for protection when an area was rid of devilish associations. To commemorate the millennium, a mosaic representing the saint was installed at the entrance to the churchyard. It is surrounded by waterwashed stones from the Lune. The doorway of the church is said to hold pieces of stone dating from the time of the Conqueror, and stonework in the churchyard includes some that was in use in the Norman period.

At Caton the Normans built a church on a mound between two becks and the village arose around the church. From time to time the becks, especially the one down Littledale, overflow dramatically. Sites of former motte and bailey structures are particularly common in the lower part of the valley.

Chapter 3

Religious Affairs

Cockersands, an abbey standing on windswept mossland near the mouth of the Lune, was originally known as St Mary of the Marsh on the Cockersand, hinting at its bleak situation. Leland, traveller and antiquary, visited Cockersands Abbey, which was 'standing veri blekely an object toal Wynddes'. The monks lived in fear of being engulfed by the sea.

Early in the 12th century, the site of the abbey had been given by William de Lancaster, 2nd Baron of Kendal and Lord of Wyresdale. Hugh Garth, 'a heremyt [hermit] of great perfeccon', is reputed to have collected the alms to finance the building of a small hospital that was attended by Canons of the Premonstratensian Order from Croxton Abbey in Leicestershire. William, the donor, made it possible for a hospital to be established for aged and infirm monks but breathed his last in 1184. Two years later the abbey owned better land in the adjacent township of Thurnam, thanks to the generosity of its lord, one William de Furness. In 1190 Cockersands, a monastery hospital, came under the protection and benefited from the support of Pope Clement III. Disputes with the Austin Canons of Leicester Abbey were resolved and Abbot Paul and the convent of Leicester gave permission for Cockersand to have the status of an abbey, but it was agreed that no further land would be acquired in the manor. Cockersands benefited from many gifts and grants, including the pasturage of Pilling and the patronage of Garstang church, and by 1292 had connections and riches in almost 200 townships.

When the plague was raging in 1363, and a sea-battered and poverty-stricken abbey was finding recruitment difficult, a hopeful note was sounded by the ordination of several canons as priests. Towards the end of May 1536, Royal Commissioners under the Act of Suppression called at Cockersands and reported that the prior and 21 canons, all of them priests, were of honest conversation and desirous to continue in religion. Two of the priests

36 *Tower of St Oswald's, Ravenstonedale.*

were associated with chantries at Tunstall and Middleton, two more were proctors for Mitton and Garstang. All four could be recalled to the abbey. Surprisingly, there was no reference to lay brothers. Abbot Poulton and his canons surrendered the house on 29 January 1539, and the site, along with the demesne lands and the Rectory of Garstang, were leased to John Burnell and Robert Gardiner for 21 years. On 1 September 1542, John Kitchen of Hatfield, Hertfordshire, who had farmed the site of the monastery from 1539, purchased it from the Crown for £700. All that remains of Cockersands Abbey, which once spread over an acre of ground and ranked third among Lancashire's monastic houses, is a chapter house. It survived because a local family used it as a private vault. It subsequently became a shelter for cattle, the place to cheat a searching wind that over many years twisted local hawthorn trees.

Near the porch of St Oswald's Church at Ravenstonedale, near the source of the Lune, a Saxon cross was revealed. On the north side of the church, the foundations of a Gilbertine abbey of around 1200 AD were excavated in 1920. The Gilbertine order of Canons Regular, founded in around 1130, was thoroughly English. The canons came to Ravenstonedale from a priory at Walton on Humberside which had been granted the valley in 1336. Belief in Christianity in this district was rock solid. Stephen Brunskill, born in 1748, introduced Wesleyanism to Orton and to a large part of Westmorland. He recalled in his autobiography that when he first went among the people

37 *Remains of Gilbertine Priory, Ravenstonedale.*

38 *Kirkby Lonsdale church, from a painting by Ralph Cox c.1838.*

he was like a speckled hen or one smitten by the plague, shunned and styled a 'Methodist', a term of derision that became respectable through his witness.

Adam Sedgwick was fond of revisiting his boyhood haunts in Dentdale and keen to uphold old ideas and ways. When a mistake at Cowgill, the topmost area, resulted in the wrong name being given to the chapel in 1868, Sedgwick wrote a slim *Memorial by the Trustees of Cowgill Chapel*. Queen Victoria, who respected the geologist, read a copy of the book and set in train the events which led to the passing of a corrective piece of legislation, the Cowgill Chapel Act of 1869, whereupon Sedgwick published a *Supplement* to his earlier book that is revered by local historians.

The upper Lune has associations with the earliest days of Quakerism. In 1652 George Fox, ascending Pendle Hill in Lancashire, 'was moved to sound the day of the Lord, and the Lord let me see in what places He had a great people to be gathered … At night we came to an inn, and declared truth to the man … Here the Lord opened unto me, and let me see great people in white raiment by a river that parted two counties.' Travelling through the dales, he sighted the River Lune. 'The next day I went to a meeting at Justice Gervase Benson's, where I met a people that were separated from the public worship. This was the place I had seen where a people came forth in white

39 *Kirkby Lonsdale churchyard.*

40 *Howgill church.*

raiment.' No contemporary portrait exists of George Fox, so we cannot know the precise appearance of the founder of Quakerism. The nearest likeness we have is a primitive woodcut dated about 1690. All later 18th- and 19th-century portrayals are doubtful.

On a market day in the following year, William Dewsbury, one of Fox's followers, chose to orate from beside the market cross at Sedbergh. As he preached, the crowd became so unruly the market cross was toppled and damaged in the fall. But the most memorable gathering took place well away from any town, on Sunday 13 June 1652. George Fox used an outcrop on Firbank Fell as a natural pulpit and preached for three hours to an estimated 1,000 people known as Seekers, all of whom experienced great spiritual power. Among them was Colonel Benson, lawyer and former Mayor of Kendal. Benson's first wife, Dorothy, heckled a priest and was imprisoned at York, where in 1653 she gave birth to a son she called Immanuel. Adjoining Fox's Pulpit is a plot of land, about a quarter of an acre in extent, which became the site of Firbank Chapel and a small school. Today a single tombstone hints at its secondary purpose.

Early Quakers held a firm belief in the equality of man: a person followed God's laws rather than those of the land; there was no doffing of hats, no payment of tithes to the Church, and no Oath of Allegiance to the King. By 1664 most of the Quakers in the national population resided in and around Sedbergh. During the lifetime of Cromwell, they were protected, but on the accession of Charles II the protection was withdrawn. The Act of Uniformity imposed the Book of Common Prayer and worship in the parish churches. Enforced attendance at what George Fox called 'steeple-houses' was unacceptable to the Quakers and their stand was in line with the outlook of independent-minded men throughout the dale country.

In 1665 the Blayklings, living at the farmstead known as Draw-well in the tucked-away village of Howgill, invited a number of Seekers to meet for worship in their barn, despite the Conventicle Act, passed in 1670, under

41 *Middleton church, Upper Lunesdale*

42 *St Peter's Church, Leck*

which a gathering of more than five people was illegal. Most of those who attended were farmers and shepherds – pious people, deeply dissatisfied with the ways and worship of the Anglican Church and looking for valid religious experience and fresh spiritual insight. The illegal meeting, held at risk of arrest and imprisonment, was for silent worship. A troop of militia under Ensign Lawrence Hodgson of Dent ordered them out of the barn and told them to walk into Sedbergh. None obeyed. Settling among the bracken fronds on a hillside, they continued their new form of worship. George Fox, staying at Draw-well in 1677, is said to have retired to a recess up a stone staircase for meditation. Close by the farmhouse is a ford over the Lune which leads to Fox's Pulpit on Firbank Fell.

43 *Sketch from the archive of the Society of Friends, of founder George Fox.*

44 *Fox's Pulpit on Firbank Fell.*

A meeting house was built, illegally, at Lower Brigflatts, a village which, at the close of the 16th century, was a fairly self-sufficient community of about 75 people relying mainly on the weaving of flax. The site was purchased at a cost of 10 shillings and the building was erected by voluntary labour. When it came into use in 1675, there was no proper floor or ceiling. Any holes that appeared were stuffed with moss and forty years elapsed before a ceiling was installed. A raised wooden floor was fitted in 1881 and, the village pond being apt to flood, a gap of 34 inches was left between the underside of the floorboards and the earth. Further additions were a wooden gallery and, there being farmers in the congregation, a dog pen. A small burial ground was purchased in 1656, the last burial taking place in recent times. Although there are only 78 headstones, records indicate there have been over 770 burials. Graves might be re-opened after a century and the surviving bones moved to one side, making room for the interment of a 'fresh' body.

The Glorious Revolution of 1688 brought William and Mary to the throne. A year later the Toleration Act gave Dissenters, as nonconformists were then known, freedom of worship. At Ravenstonedale a licensed meeting house lay within the home of George Parkin, and in 1690 the minister appointed was Timothy Punshon, who was granted by the Presbyterian Fund 'above £20 per annum besides the £8 per annum given by Lord Wharton'. The land was purchased for £100. In 1726, during the ministry of Mr Magee, a proper meeting house was built. In troubled times, between 1817 and 1867, the Rev. William Hasell went over to the Wesleyans, taking with him a great part of the congregation. The chapel was reconstituted in 1838, four women and two men forming the new Society.

Early ministers and congregation were at loggerheads for a variety of reasons, mainly doctrinal. James Muscutt in 1811 accepted the call to minister here only 'upon condition that the Church be reorganised and put

45 *The only upright tombstone in a roadside burial ground near Fox's Pulpit.*

46 *Brigflatts Meeting House, near Sedbergh.*

47 *High Chapel, Ravenstonedale.*

upon the Independent or Congregational plan', a less centralised form of church government than Presbyterianism. In the short but fruitful ministry of Muscutt at the High Chapel a little belfry was erected. The shrill monitor bell was intended to 'bring the people in, and about the same time, which by the blessing of God answers the end designed'.

In 1828 Parliament passed an Act that substantially eased the restrictions on freedom of worship by Dissenters, but it was still necessary for nonconformist places of worship to be registered with the Bishop of the appropriate Diocese. At Ravenstonedale in 1838, during the ministry of the Rev. John Hessel, there was a shock when he left Independency to become an adherent of John Wesley. Most of the congregation left also and a Wesleyan Chapel was built lower down the village street. Life at the High Chapel was maintained by a faithful few. In 1972 the Presbyterian Church of England and the Congregational Church in England and Wales set aside the differences of three centuries to become, by Act of Parliament, the United Reformed Church.

John Wesley visited Kendal in April 1753, preaching in a room where Mr Ingham's society met. Wesley was 'a little disgusted' when people arrived and sat down without preliminary prayer. They also sat during the hymn;

48 *Isolated Methodist chapel in the parish of Stonesdale, near Sedbergh.*

they knew the tune but did not join in the singing. The first local Methodist Chapel was opened in Kirkby Lonsdale in 1835. The Rev. David McNicholl and the Rev. William O. Booth preached at the opening services, travelling to Kirkby Lonsdale from Liverpool, an arduous journey in pre-railway days. In 1929 the Kendal Circuit stationed an ordained minister at Kirkby Lonsdale, the arrangement lasting for a decade. In 1938 the junior minister was moved to Milnthorpe. From 1946 to 1949 a lay pastor resided in Kirkby Lonsdale.

At Sedbergh in the early 19th century an itinerant tea retailer called Jonathan Kershaw made a number of converts in the town. Among them was Thomas Herd. He was mainly responsible for the building, in 1805, of the first Wesleyan Chapel hereabouts. Primitive Methodists became locally active in 1822. The Wesleyans of Sedbergh, dissatisfied with the ministerial attention they received from Kendal, formed the Hawes and Sedbergh Circuit in 1871, largely financed by one Christopher Taylor. In 1864 the old chapel had run into considerable debt, but it was decided to work on a new one. Octagonal in style, and costing around £1,000, the striking new building was opened in 1865.

William Moister, a native of Sedbergh who became a Wesleyan minister and a missionary, helped raise the money for the new chapel. By 1871 he was playing a leading part in the formation of the new Sedbergh Circuit, becoming its first Superintendent Minister. He worked for no financial reward and, indeed, covered the cost of building a house for the Superintendent Minister together with his wife. Soon after the turn of the century most of the structure was demolished, the octagonal chapel being unsuited to enlargement, but the windows were retained. Work began on building the present chapel just before the First World War, and it opened its doors on 23 October 1914.

In Garsdale, off-shoot of the upper Lune, an Anglican church dedicated to St John was built in 1861 on the site of a medieval chapel described by Coleridge to his friend Wordsworth as 'a lowly house of prayer in a charming little valley'. The 'lowly house' was demolished in the year its successor was built. Garsdale, with numerous chapels, rang with Methodist praise. A Yorkshire Television film of the 1970s featured Grisedale, a subsidiary, as *The Dale that Died*, and dealt with some of the spiritual descendants of an evangelist called Richard Atkinson. He had humble beginning but re-invigorated local Methodism; he was both 'saved' and 'saving'. Garsdale had three places of worship, Low Smithy and Garsdale Street, where there is the largest concentration of buildings at The Street, and a third chapel, of Primitive Methodist origins and known as Junction Chapel, at the dalehead where the Settle-Carlisle Railway branched into the Wensleydale line. The foundation stone of this chapel was laid by Reuben Alton, one of a family that arrived at the railway station cottages from Leeds. Junction Chapel is unusual, a single room occupying an isolated if roadside position close to the Settle-Carlisle railway. It is said that 106 people gathered in this tiny chapel on Good Friday 1983, and afterwards they tucked into a supper of the Jacob's Join variety, each person contributing food to a common pool.

The present church at Leck, dating from 1915, stands on the site of three earlier churches. Its predecessor was gutted by a fire that began when a lamp was inadvertently left burning after organ practice. Now there is a fine Harrison & Harrison organ. The 'blower house' is situated near the kissing-gate in the graveyard and air is pumped underground, between the graves, to the organ. In the graveyard are buried three young girls from the Clergy Daughters' School that was established at Cowan Bridge in 1824. They fell victim to the low fever (typhus) that periodically decimated the school and also claimed many lives in the district.

Today Kirkby Lonsdale and its environs form the Rainbow parish, comprising the seven original churches with each having one colour from the rainbow. The Rainbow title was given to an early Team Ministry, formed in 1976. The concept included care for the local schools. When Preston Patrick joined the Team Ministry in 2004 the Rainbow acquired an eighth colour.

Chapter 4

Market Towns

Two historic market towns, Kirkby Lonsdale and Sedbergh, lie within the upper Lune area. T.D. Whitaker, in his *Richmondshire*, described Kirkby Lonsdale as being 'on a plain above the Lune, sufficiently elevated to command the soft foreground, where that river, already majestic and powerful, makes a graceful curve about a peninsula of meadow and pasture, exuberantly fertile and spotted with standard forest trees'. The 'soft scene' contrasts with 'the noblest of backgrounds', comprising 'the long ridge of Gray Garth [Gragareth], the towering height of Ingleborough to the south-east, and the piked points of Howgill to the north'. Kirkby Lonsdale is today located in Cumbria but stands close to the borders of North Yorkshire and Lancashire. With one third of local homes being detached, and a selection of shops both traditional and modern, the town is a favoured place of residence and has a current population of 2,500. The Queen Elizabeth School, with 1,400 pupils drawn from the locality and from North Yorkshire and Lancashire, is the largest employer in the town.

The name Kirkby Lonsdale indicates the presence of a church above an important fording point of the Lune. All three elements of the name are from the Norse period. The settlement evolved beside a convenient crossing point of the Lune. A tract of level ground from the top of Mill Brow was the main point of access. Thirteen miles south-east of Kendal, the town grew steadily and quietly, having a church by Saxon times and being referred to in the Domesday Survey of 1086 as *Cherkeby Lownesdale* – church town of Lunesdale.

In 1093 the Saxon church was gifted to St Mary's Abbey at York by Ivo de Taillebois, the Baron of Kendal. Abbot's Hall in the Swinemarket is a venerable building that has evolved from the premises wherein agents appointed by St Mary's Abbey collected tithes and dealt with local disputes.

49 *Kirkby Lonsdale from Casterton Low Lodge in 1849.*

In a valuation of church livings made by Pope Nicholas IV in 1291, the church was assessed at 130 marks and the Vicarage at 24 marks. The church was almost certainly ravaged in the raids that followed the Scottish victory at Bannockburn in 1314. The stone church provided by St Mary's Abbey was, with several extensions, the most impressive of 60 parish churches originating in Cumbria during the 12th century. Following the Dissolution, Abbey property reverted to the Crown, specifically Henry VIII. In about 1550 Queen Mary presented the holdings of the former abbey to Trinity College, Cambridge, under whose patronage the church exists today.

A clock fitted in 1560 lacked a dial, the hour being struck on a single bell. In 1710, work was undertaken on the top part of the tower and a hole was left in a 5ft thick wall for the clock, which was subsequently set off-centre. It was then possible for it to be seen throughout the length of Church Street. The bell-ringers had a thirsty job. As well as the effort with the bell ropes, there was the initial toil up spiral stone steps. The Ringer's Orders are presented in the form of a rhyme:

If to ring ye do come here
You must ring well with Hand and Ear.
Keep stroke, and time, and go not out
Or else you'll forfeit without a doubt.
He that a bell doth overthrow,
Must pay his groat before he go.
He that rings with his hat on,
Must pay his groat and so be gone,
He that rings with spur on heel,
The same penalty he must feel.
If an oath you chance to hear,
You forfeit each two quarts of beer.
These lines are old, they are not new.

Inevitably the church suffered from Victorian restoration, the cost being met by the Earl of Bective. The roof line was raised and the building acquired battlements. When the Rev. A.P. Kirkpatrick was vicar, a service was held at 7.30 a.m. every day of the week, winter and summer alike. During the Second World War, after-dark services were illuminated by two candles on

50 *Kirkby Lonsdale Market Place in 1855.*

51 *The Lune at Sandy Beds from the Lady's Well in 1849.*

the altar table. Mr Benjamin Shaw, parish clerk for over thirty years, missed only two services, both through ill health. In recent times a discarded font, used for years as a trough on a farm, was restored to the church.

Pevsner considered Kirkby Lonsdale worth visiting for the church alone. Visitors marvel at the massive columns supporting the north arcade, which are carved with a version of trellis decoration like that in Durham Cathedral. There is a Norman arch beneath the tower. Kirkby Lonsdale Vicarage dates from 1783. A third storey was added in the 1830s by a clergyman who was meeting the needs of his large family. From 1889 until 1908 the elegant building housed the Rev. Llewellyn-Davies, his wife and five sons, who inspired J.M. Barrie to write *Peter Pan*. After the reverend gentlemen and his wife died, Barrie assumed responsibility for the education of the sons. A gazebo, moved from its original position and much altered, is seen by those heading for The Brow, a walkway offering an admirable view of the valley. It is an outstanding viewpoint. In the picture is Casterton Fell and, distantly, Ingleborough. A sweep of park-like landscape was praised by

Ruskin and painted by Turner. Kirfitt Hall (1625), which lies across the river, was, according to local tradition, built on the site of an earlier house at which Henry VIII stayed when courting Katharine Parr, whose home was Kendal Castle.

J.M.W. Turner and John Ruskin, two men of strong artistic inclination, stood at the edge of the churchyard, near where the land plunges away to the Lune, and drew general attention to what was to become celebrated as Ruskin's View. Turner was touring the north country in 1816, making sketches for a projected *General History of the County of York* by Dr Thomas Dunham Whitaker. On the death of Whitaker the work was incomplete, and rather more than a score of Turner's sketches appeared in a history of Richmondshire and another tome featuring picturesque views of England and Wales which were published in the 1820s. Ruskin championed the works of Turner, and became one of his executors with regard to classified paintings that Turner left to the nation. He makes enthusiastic reference to the View

52 *The Lune From the N.E. Corner of Kirkby Lonsdale Churchyard, by J.M.W. Turner, from an engraving of 1822.*

in *Fors Clavigera* (1875): 'The Valley of the Lune at Kirkby is one of the loveliest scenes in England – therefore in the world. Whatever moorland hill, sweet river and English forest foliage can be at their best, is gathered there; and chiefly seen from the steep bank which falls to the stream side from the upper part of the town itself ... I do not know in all my own country, still less in France and Italy, a place more naturally divine or a more priceless possession of true "Holy Land".' Ruskin then railed against ways in which the viewpoint had been desecrated, referring to a fence formed of iron railings and some 'clumsy hardware', namely iron seats with serpentine decoration.

Life at Kirkby Lonsdale in more modern times was recalled by Alexander Pearson when, in 1945, he lay in a Manchester nursing home after a surgical operation. Pondering on his long life, he sent to the stationer's for some exercise books and wrote in them 'such tales of my ancestors and accounts of my personal doings as I thought might be of interest to the members of my family'. For 40 years *The Doings of a Country Solicitor* have charmed anyone who has more than a passing interest in the upper Lune. Alexander lived at Abbots Brow, the gardens of which he designed and developed, extending the garden almost to the river. The charm of his book lies in its

portrayal of social life at the turn of the century, and especially the big estates which were major employers of local labour. Wilson Goad recalls that when he was apprenticed to a solicitor he was recommended to Alexander Pearson as someone who might type out the latter's manuscript. He did the work at the rate of threepence a folio. It was typed several times before being considered ready for the printer.

The book was published privately, by subscription, the author dedicating it to Thersa Hothersall, a nurse who read the first pages and encouraged him to write more. Forty years after its first appearance, a second edition of the book was launched. The event took place at the offices of Pearson and Pearson, overlooking the Market Place at Kirkby Lonsdale, where Pearson became an articled clerk in 1888.

53 *A notice attached to the wall of the old Royal Hotel in the Market Place at Kirkby Lonsdale.*

He eventually succeeded his father as head of the firm which continues to occupy premises overlooking Market Place. It moved to the present main office in 1919, prior to which an office by the church was occupied. Alexander Pearson's experiences do not dominate the book but he tells us that at Kirkby Lonsdale his advice was sought on a variety of social matters. A mother asked him whether or not her daughter should be allowed to visit a named country house, whispers having reached her of 'carryings on' at some of the weekend parties. We also read that one tenant, at the mention of 'unpopular' landlords, would remark, 'Aye, there's eniew [enough] of a few.' A Victorian postmaster at Kirkby Lonsdale recalled by Alexander gave short shrift to a visitor staying at Underley Hall. The visitor needed to send urgent information to London and an acknowledgement of its receipt was required. The message was encoded to ensure secrecy. A groom took it the post office so it might be telegraphed and waited for the reply. None came and the groom asked for an explanation. The postmaster was unable to make sense of the message and had not despatched it, commenting, 'Folk that want telegrams sending shouldn't write such stuff.'

54 *Ruskin's View, Kirkby Lonsdale.*

55   *Devil's Bridge (by Edward Jeffrey).*

When Pevsner paid a brief but perceptive visit to Kirkby Lonsdale, he wrote of it as 'a town of dark grey stone houses enjoyable to wander through and indeed nowhere not enjoyable'. The dark grey stone was local limestone. Towards the end of the 15th century, or early in the following century, when the wool trade reached its commercial peak, this was an important wool town. So was Kendal, whose motto was 'Wool is My Bread'. Kirkby Lonsdale had an extensive rebuilding phase during the late 17th and early 18th centuries. Mitchelgate, a principal road, was transformed, the thatched cottages demolished and replaced by dwellings of stone roofed with slate. The main streets of the little town had their cobbles replaced by smoother surfaces. Norman Nicholson, the Cumbrian poet, wrote in 1963 that the use of limestone rather than slate gave Kirkby Lonsdale more of the look of Tudor England. Here were narrow streets and secluded squares and, Nicholson added, 'Along the main street there is scarcely a house, an inn or a shop which does not give pleasure in its shape and companionableness.'

Kirkby Lonsdale received a market charter from Henry III in 1227. The grant, for a weekly market and an annual fair, was made to John de Kirkeby in Lounesdale and his successors. A run of fairs ended well over a century ago, but

56 *Kirkby Lonsdale market cross in its new position.*

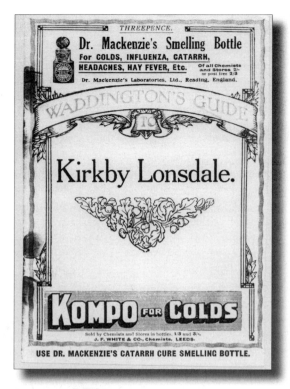

THREEPENCE.

Dr. Mackenzie's Smelling Bottle

For COLDS, INFLUENZA, CATARRH,
HEADACHES, HAY FEVER, Etc.   Of all Chemists
and Stores 2/-
or post free 2/3

Dr. Mackenzie's Laboratories, Ltd., Reading, England.

WADDINGTON'S GUIDE

Kirkby Lonsdale.

KOMPO FOR COLDS

Sold by Chemists and Stores in bottles, 1/3 and 3/-.
J. F. WHITE & CO., Chemists, LEEDS.

USE DR. MACKENZIE'S CATARRH CURE SMELLING BOTTLE.

57   *Cover of Early Guide to Kirkby Lonsdale.*

lives on in the name of Fairbank which, extending from near the church, was once the northern extremity of the town and the start of the older, steeper, road to Kendal. The medieval market cross has been moved and since 1819 has been the central feature of the Swinemarket. The writer of *Waddington's Guide to Kirkby Lonsdale* (published in York and undated) noted that, in common with many other country towns in the north, Kirkby consisted chiefly of a long street 'along which the coaches plied in its palmier days on their journeys between Settle and Kendal. A few lesser streets branch off on either side, leading to nowhere in particular ... Kirkby Lonsdale has been described as a fair specimen of those old-world spots ... which stand apart from the bustling world and retain their ancient characteristics in spite of the changing tendencies of the age.'

The Market Square was laid out early in the 1820s, largely at the behest of the Earl of Lonsdale, lord of the manor. It had previously been the garden of Jackson's Hall, the site of which was to be taken over by the *Royal Hotel.* For many years it was an open space that lived up to its name. On market days pens were set up for sheep, cattle displayed the docility of their breed, and children found pleasure in swings that had been specially erected. The central feature of the Market Square is the Butter Cross, of vaguely medieval appearance although it was built as recently as 1905 to commemorate the wife of the Rev. J. Llewellyn-Davies, the local vicar. Initially it was ornate and surmounted by eight upper ogee ribs with a cross at the peak. These were removed sixty years ago because in danger of collapse from traffic vibration and the ageing state of the stone which had not been of especially good quality when cut. Norman Nicholson described the Market Square as being 'cluttered by an excessively ugly market cross, built in the form of a crown and acting now [1963] as a bus shelter'.

58 *Bective Road Archway, Kirkby Lonsdale.*

Thursday is market day. A census of 1841, when the little town was thriving, put the local population at about 1,500. The market was held in the open streets and involved the sale of cattle, sheep, horses, pigs, goats and poultry. Additionally there were five annual fairs, and over 100 tradesmen of all types had premises in the town, and from it or through it operated 33 carriers and 19 coaches. Being a calling point for drovers, packhorse trains and horse-drawn coaches, Kirkby Lonsdale was well-endowed with inns and ale-houses, their 17th-century names, *Sun*, *Red Dragon*, *Green Dragon*, *Fleece* and *King's Arms*, evoking the old days. At the last named, which formed part of a block of buildings known as Kirkby Hall, could be found 'Drunken Barnaby', a rhymester in Latin who

> came to Lonsdale, where I stand
> At Hall, into a tavern made,
> Neat gates, white walls – nought was sparing,
> Pots brimful – no thought of caring;
> They, drink, laugh; are still mirth-making,
> Nought they see that's worth care-taking.

The *Rose and Crown Inn* was destroyed by fire on 6 December 1820, five young women sleeping at the house being burned to death. A commemorative obelisk was erected in the churchyard, and on the site, in 1822, was built the *Royal Hotel*, the name referring to Queen Adelaide, widow of William IV,

who broke a journey to the Lake District here on 23 July 1840. The *Royal*, which dominates the Market Square, had its heyday during the term of Old John Wilman, who had an enormous staff and, behind the premises, stabling sufficient for 65 fine horses of various types. On market day visiting farmers left their horses here, and those who stopped overnight at the *Royal* had their horses rested and fed. A lad who began his working life 'mucking out' at the stables might go on to become a groom, then a coachman, at a notable local house such as Underley Hall.

When Queen Victoria's Diamond Jubilee was celebrated with national rejoicing on 20 June 1897, the Market Square was suitably decorated, and the

59 *The Gazebo, Kirkby Lonsdale churchyard.*

commemorative procession included Dr W.S. Paget-Tomlinson, High Sheriff, in his splendid coach, and a company of the 2nd (Westmorland) Volunteer Battalion of the Border Regiment. The County Yeomanry of Westmorland and Cumberland had a local Troop which, on St George's Day, or the nearest Sunday, paraded through the town. Headed by a brass band, the Troopers marched to church in full dress of scarlet and gold with white braid. An annual training camp took place at Lowther Park, courtesy of Lord Lonsdale, who for many years commanded the Regiment. The Volunteers had an annual ball at Kirkby Lonsdale, and on show day presented a round of military sports.

Until the Second World War the streets at Kirkby echoed to the clatter of horses' hooves on cobbles, and on market day the square was packed with carts on which lay farm produce of all kinds. Horses had a hard life, being over-driven, and many were soon knocking their legs together. Retailers of milk used a type of pony that became known as a 'milk galloway'. The butcher, with a heavier load for the animal to haul, wanted a horse of about 15 hands. The doctor had a good class of half-thoroughbred, a horse that might get away fast; he employed a coachman to stand by horse and trap while he attended to his patients. Every horse owner had a field. The old names endure

60 *Devil's Bridge, Kirkby Lonsdale (from* Thomas Pennant's Tour, *1801).*

although there might not have been a horse in the field for many years. Some of the land is now covered by housing estates. Jonty Wilson recalled the Doctor's Field, the Vet's Field and one named after Dales the butchers. None of the fields exceeded five acres. In winter, when the horses were indoors, the land was usually let to farmers for grazing sheep.

61 *Alley at Kirkby Lonsdale.*

The market at Kirkby Lonsdale suffered when an auction mart was opened. Highly mechanised dairies also cut out the profit formerly made by the middle-man. As transport connections improved, people began to travel to the larger indoor markets at the big towns, and after the First World War there were no stalls on market day for over two decades. All market dues went to the Earl of Lonsdale until 1932, after which they were claimed by the South Westmorland Rural District Council, who retained a third, the remainder being split between the County Council, for the upkeep of the approach road, and the Parish Council.

Kirkby Lonsdale acquired a by-pass, flanked by chestnut trees, which took most of the transport pressure off the centre. The town's cosy feel was compromised by the construction of a roundabout giving access to a supermarket and adjacent car parks, and opening up the town from the west, but the visitor still has a view of slate roofs, greystone masonry, green hills and, distantly, flat-topped Ingleborough. For two days each September, Kirkby Lonsdale is in gala mood for a Victorian Fair. Victorian garb is worn, stalls are erected by traders, crafts are demonstrated, and there is outdoor entertainment. A highlight is a service in the historic church. Kirkby Lonsdale has three times been the national winner of the Britain in Bloom (small country town section) competition.

Sedbergh, the largest town in the Yorkshire Dales National Park, developed at the confluence of four rivers and is sandwiched between Winder, a 1,551ft outlier of the Howgill Fells, and the River Rawthey, boisterous tributary of the Lune. The Rawthey has its source on Baugh Fell. Approach roads to Sedbergh are inclined to be narrow, with tall, flanking hedges.

62 *James Thompson, auctioneer, Kirkby Lonsdale.*

They owe their height and luxuriance to something other than the procrastination of farmers, mild weather filtering up from the Irish Sea and providing high humidity in the upper valley.

The town's name derives from the the Norse *Set Berg* (a flat-topped hill) or *Sadda's Berg* (the fortified hill of a Saxon named Sadda). The Normans, after subjecting much of the north country to fire and sword, held onto their new possessions, in part, by constructing fortifications of the motte and bailey type. The chosen site – that flat-topped hill – is still known as Castlehaw though it is now simply a mound shaped like an upturned pudding basin. During the Second World War this eminence held a lookout that was manned by members of the Royal Observer Corps. On early maps, and on plate belonging to St Andrew's Church, the town's name is rendered 'Sedber', and old folk refer to 'Sebber Town'. The Normans built a church in about 1130. Was the choice of Andrew as patron saint an attempt to placate another despoiler, the rampaging Scots? A modern representation of the saint, backed by his traditional diagonal cross, occupies a niche over the church's outer door.

63 *Sedbergh (by Frank Armstrong).*

64 *Sedbergh on Market Day, c.1980.*

The town lies at the meeting place of four valleys. Freda Trott, local historian, likened its situation to the palm of an outstretched hand, the thumb pointing north towards Howgill and fingers spreading along the dales towards Cautley, Garsdale, Dent and Lunesdale. Sedbergh is long, narrow and compact and has a pinched appearance, its main thoroughfare being at one point 11 feet wide and giving rise to 'six abreast Sebba', derived from the notion that street and pavements were filled by six people walking abreast. For one day in August, when the Charter Market takes place, Main Street is closed, and stalls line the street. William Riley, the Yorkshire novelist, arriving at Sedbergh in 1939 observed, 'It is not often that you find in any town or village a street so narrow that conveyances cannot pass each other; and as this street is also a main road, the congestion here in summer-time is something to marvel at.' Extending from the main street are alleys which beg to be explored. Small courtyards are flanked by buildings that at one time had industrial value, upstairs galleries being used mainly for spinning wool.

The district being too bleak for grain crops, the food market was limited to staple items such as oatmeal until the arrival of the railway in 1863. An auction mart is situated by the road to Kendal. Sedbergh's industrial phase began in the last decade of the 18th century with the construction of mills at Howgill, Birks and Millthrop where wool from the backs of local sheep was processed locally. A woollen mill at Hebblethwaite Hall (1792) was succeeded by Farfield Mill (1837), its looms powered by the waters of the Clough, the river of Garsdale. Until the early part of the 19th century, the narrow main street was adequate for the packhorses setting off for Kendal with wool and cloth provided by local industry, and with knitted items such as hosiery, long stockings and caps. Local roads were turnpiked in the 1760s. In 1823, when the *King's Arms* at Sedbergh was advertised for sale, it was 'the only Posting-house there, and on the newly established road from Liverpool to Newcastle'.

For much of its history, Sedbergh occupied the northern edge of the West Riding of Yorkshire and Wakefield was the county town. In the mid-18th century, when there was no acting magistrate within fifty miles, local people pleaded to be exempted from jury service in York by reason of the town's 'far remoteness'. At the revision of county boundaries in 1974, the town was included in the new county of Cumbria but remained within the bounds of the Yorkshire Dales National Park. Three points had been made to the Boundary Commission to justify keeping the town in Yorkshire: West Riding County Council had always exercised efficient administration; ancient and jealously guarded loyalties should not be set aside, except for overwhelming reasons; and at no time had there been any difficulty in obtaining county councillors to undertake their duties. But the points were made in vain. Prior to 1974 Yorkshire had ended at a bridge over Carlingill Beck, which emanates from the western side of the Howgills, although a stranger would not have guessed it for the stone marking the county boundary had been deliberately defaced during the Second World War. When the M6 opened, Sedbergh lay only four and a half miles from the new motorway.

Piecemeal development of Sedbergh church over several centuries has led to a lack of symmetry. A five-light window on the east wall is not in a central position, and a single large picture depicting the call of Christ to Andrew and brother Peter, his fishing partner, is spread over the full width of the five lights. Major restoration of the church was undertaken in 1886 under the direction of Austin and Paley, who were then involved in extensive work for Sedbergh School. New woodwork – stalls, pews, pulpit – were the work of Waring and Gillow of Lancaster. In recent years, the church has been shared with Roman Catholics.

65 *Sedbergh from the churchyard.*

66 *Sedbergh church from the School's cricket field.*

Eleven years after the restoration of the church a wooden building that had served as a chapel at Sedbergh School was replaced by an imposing new chapel, in the Perpendicular style of architecture, at a cost of £7,826 12s. Sedbergh School is largely responsible for the modern shape of the town, its substantial buildings not arranged in a huddle, like many schools, but separated by broad green spaces. A public school was founded in 1525 by Dr Roger Lupton, a native of Howgill who was keen to increase the 'learning in Christ's church' for 'for his soul's health'. Lupton became a Canon of Windsor and Provost of Eton. The school was a chantry school, the land on which it stood having been granted by Coverham Abbey. Ultimately, it became a free grammar school. It was well enough known for William Wordsworth to enrol his son. William's wife, Mary (née Hutchinson) had relations at the school.

Sedbergh has been a market town for over seven centuries. A charter for markets and fairs was granted to Lady Alice de Staveley by Henry III in 1251 and permitted an annual fair to be held 'on the Even and for the Feast of the Nativity of St Mary'. The Staveleys, descended from Danish noblemen who had been settled in the north country for many years, arrived in Sedbergh via Staveley near Knaresborough, having become lords of the manors of Sedbergh, Garsdale and Dent. Alice's father, Adam de Staveley, was clerk in the chancery of King John. Ingmire Hall, the local stately home, was the ancestral seat of the Otways and Upton families prior to its sale in 1922 and destruction by fire in 1928. Sir John Otway (1620-93) helped with the restoration of King Charles II and also lent his support to the burgeoning Quaker movement.

In 2005, when Sedbergh was in commercial decline, it was re-born as a 'book town', the sale of books becoming a prime feature of eight local businesses. Since that year, a Festival of Literature and Drama has been held annually.

67 *Sketch of Sedbergh's main street.*

Chapter 5

Affluent Estates

Victorian Lunesdale was shaped and beautified by the creation of large estates and palatial country houses. The main estates, Underley, Biggins, Rigmaden and Lunefield, had a profound effect on local life and set the tone of the district. Underley owned virtually three-quarters of Kirkby Lonsdale and employed about three-quarters of the local men. The estate's bankers were the prestigious Farrer and Co. of London. The town of Kirkby Lonsdale burgeoned as long as Underley and other estates supplied a demand for labour, goods and services. Lower down the valley, a grand lifestyle was enjoyed at places such as Hornby Castle and Capernwray Hall. Alexander Pearson, solicitor of Kirkby Lonsdale, attending a ball at Hornby Castle, noticed that footmen had powdered hair. When dining at Capernwray Hall, 'you did so à la carte, choosing what you fancied from the menu and eating it there and then, even though it might be a savoury and the others were having their soup. If you wished to sit up until morning and have a meal before retiring you would not be upsetting the household. A night staff was on duty.' Wealthy owners also endowed the district with schools and churches, several of the latter being designed by the revered Lancaster firm of Austin and Paley.

Underley, a palatial building close to Kirkby Lonsdale, lay in a vast park within a sweep of the Lune and had a backdrop of the Middleton Fells. The name had been derived from the surname of Ughtred de Underley, a former landowner. He received from the Abbey of St Mary at York a grant of 15 acres and one rood of land. A mansion, with its hundred rooms, was constructed on the site of an earlier hall for Alexander Nowell, a member of an old Yorkshire family and former Army Officer in India, where he had made a fortune which was largely devoted to the construction of Underley. Work began in 1825 and was completed six years later, along with a small

68 *Underley Hall from the Casterton Woods in 1849.*

estate. During the construction period, Nowell had a temporary residence in Kirkby Lonsdale; it became Nos 5 and 7 Fairbank. (No. 5 was occupied, in due course, by General Wyatt, who 'chose' the Unknown Soldier for the memorial in Westminster Abbey after the First World War.) The Hall was designed by Webster of Kendal, a pupil of William Atkinson. He had an extensive country house practice in the north, favouring symmetry, and was a pioneer of the 'Jacobean' style of architecture. At Underley he used yellow freestone and the Georgian square plan, with some bold Tudor-style features and embellishments of his own design.

The hall was ready for occupation in 1832. The enlarged Underley estate, put on the market in 1840 at an asking price of £120,000, was bought by William Thompson, a member of an old Westmorland family who was by now a wealthy London merchant. Like Dick Whittington, Thompson left a rural area for the City, acquired a fortune and became Lord Mayor of London. He had a busy political life and was for a time a director of the Bank of England. Thompson had already bought land and property in his native county, purchasing estates at Killington in 1829. He 'retired to work', keeping up some of his London connections, and was Member of Parliament for Westmorland from 1840 until his death in 1854. Thompson's daughter, Amelia, married into the Taylour (Bective) family. Lord Bective, the 3rd Marquis of Headfort, was also to become MP for Westmorland. In the 1870s Underley was embellished on a grand scale. The Hall was extended outwards and also upwards, with a 100ft high tower. The new conservatory had a roof of wrought-iron and glass which was crowned by a glass dome and was 70 feet long, 20 feet wide and 12 feet in diameter. Lighting for the Hall was provided by a gasometer erected near the Home Farm at a cost of over £2,500. Bridging the River Lune cost £13,000.

Lord and Lady Bective's daughter, Olivia Caroline Amelia, was married in 1892 to Lord Henry Cavendish-Bentinck, half-brother of the Duke of Portland. When the Earl of Bective died in the following year, his widow took up residence at Lunefield, a manor house in the district, and the Cavendish-Bentincks moved into Underley Hall in 1901. All the property came to Lady Bentinck on her mother's death. Although he lived up to everyone's idea of a rich country squire, Lord Henry was not a pompous man. His used his London residence in Eaton Square as a base for lively social occasions at Christmas, Easter and in the summer. At other times he was able to be himself at his vast estate in the Lune Valley.

69 *A lodge at Underley Hall.*

He was interested in its everyday affairs. The farm buildings, set well away from the Hall and approached by a separate road, were substantial and eye-catching. Workmen and their families were valued. When a man was no longer able to work, he retained his cottage and was provided with a pension. His lordship had a fine herd of Shorthorn cattle, the Underley strain evolving from an animal that had been bought in Canada for the staggering sum of £9,000. Only once did his lordship sell a female from the strain. Then, uneasy about what he had done, he promptly bought it back! He ran one of the farms himself with the practical help of a bailiff. The enterprise was not profitable, though it did produce some prize-winning Shorthorn cattle. For local farmers, his efforts were a source of amusement, especially when he decided that ultra-violet glass should be fitted to windows in the shippons.

Though he knew the tenant farmers and their families, and often chatted with them, his lordship had little understanding of the lot of ordinary people. Calling at Jonty Wilson's smithy in Fairbank, Lord Henry would ask, 'Now then, Jonty, what have you got to tell me?' Jonty had no specific ties with the estate and was on easy terms with its owner so would reply, 'Your horses are a darned sight better looked after and housed than half your tenants.' When Lord Henry boomed, 'Oh, rubbish!' in reply, he was invited by Jonty to inspect some of the estate houses.

A country squire naturally took part in field sports. The slaughter of red grouse was based mainly on Deeside, a fine shooting lodge updale from the village of Dent. The shooting season opened in grand style with a cavalcade of horse-drawn vehicles from Underley along the narrow roads to the grand house near the dalehead. The woodland and rhododendron groves at Underley provided cover for around 15,000 pheasants. In pens around Terrybank Tarn were reared some 5,000 duck. Lady Cavendish-Bentink, who was shy, ran the house. Lord Henry was an outdoor man and in autumn, when pheasant shooting began, he swaggered forth with gun and dog at heel. To the Underley covert shoot came well-connected friends, and Underley Hall was big enough to accommodate them, their wives and their servants. An augmented labour force ensured that the hand-reared birds were flushed according to plan. The shoot lasted three days in November and a special train was laid on between London and Kirkby Lonsdale.

On 19 to 21 November 1913, the guns were Lord Basil Blackwood, Lord Richard Cavendish, the Earl of Kerry, Lord Henry Bentinck, Captain Lindsay, Mr M.F. Mildmay, Sir H. Shaw-Stewart, the Hon. E. Ward and Mr Jos Gibson. They slew 3,500 pheasants, 189 hares, 182 rabbits and three woodcock. Pheasant shooting ended with two 'mopping up' days, as they were known to the gamekeepers, invitations having been extended mainly to local people

70 *The tower at Underley Hall.*

and friends staying at the Hall. Lord Henry, who was regarded as a good shot, injured a shoulder and retired from the sport in 1930, and pheasant-rearing lapsed three years later. When Lord Henry died, his widow, who had no stomach for shooting, made no special effort to keep a stock of pheasants on the estate. He tried fishing, the Lune being an excellent river for trout and salmon, but lacked patience and skill and it was said only one salmon was ever hooked. That was snagged accidentally. After fishing all day, his lordship strode fretfully from the river, dragging his line behind him. On its course through the water it 'caught' a fine fish.

Hunting was undertaken with 'covert hacks' which the owners rode from the house to where the hounds were assembled. The 'hacks' were then exchanged for 'hunters'. During the London Season four Russian stallions were kept for drawing the carriage. At Underley, Brougham horses and hacks and three post-horses maintained a shuttle service between the Hall and the town. On the first journey, the mail was collected, this being available from 6 a.m. Horses and coach returned to town later in the morning for the newspapers, and a further journey was undertaken for shopping. In late Victorian times, an annual staff dinner was held at the *Royal* in Kirkby Lonsdale. More than twenty people might be staying in the house, each with many retainers, so the amount of food consumed was impressive. The Home Farm provided from six to eight Herdwick wethers a week, and local butchers supplied other types of meat. The estate gamekeepers and the Home Farm also provided the kitchen with a plentiful supply of game, ducks, geese, turkeys, guinea fowl and poultry.

His lordship, being a prominent Conservative and ruling councillor of the Kendal Habitation of the Primrose League, allowed the terrace at Underley to be used for a fête in support of the League. He and his wife were also keen on rock gardening, and counted among their friends an expert rock gardener, Reginald Farrer of Ingleborough Hall, Clapham, whose books and lectures had popularised this form of gardening. Farrer travelled a good deal in Asia, financed in part by those who received the seeds he collected. Lord Henry was one of those who funded him. The Cavendish-Bentincks had an alpine and heather rockery on the Casterton bank of the Lune, and to visit it one had to cross the river on a hand-cranked catamaran. But the land on which the rockery stood was subject to flooding and most of the original garden was eventually washed away.

During the First World War Lord Henry served in a cavalry regiment and fought at Gallipoli. Lady Henry allowed the Hall to be used as a convalescent home for soldiers. They occupied what had been the servants' quarters and the numerous guest-rooms. When life at Underley got back on a peacetime footing, fewer servants were employed. The Cavendish-Bentincks still provided lavish dinner parties, one of which, in 1927, was attended by Edward, Prince of Wales. He left the hall at 9 p.m. and staff and servants lined the drive to wave him off. Lord Henry died in 1931 and his wife in 1939. Two years later Underley Hall was sold, and during the Second World War it was used to accommodate evacuees from Bournmouth. It was then successively a girls' school, a Roman Catholic seminary and, latterly, a special school for young people.

Another huge private house in the locality was The Biggins, unofficially known as the Mansion. It was home to the Tomlinsons for about three centuries. A generation grew up without issue, two sons and two daughters remaining unmarried until Elizabeth, the youngest, was taken ill during a visit to the family's commercial interests in the dock area of Liverpool. She

71 *Outbuildings, Underley Hall.*

72 *Façade, Underley Hall.*

was attended by a Dr Paget. Two years later, when she had the only other illness of her life, the good doctor was summoned again. They married. The estate passed to the Pagets who added their name to that of the well-known family, Paget-Tomlinsons entering the social life of the Lune Valley in 1895. The owner acquired properties in Kirkby Lonsdale and on the farmland round about. Financial support was bestowed on church, Institute and local schools. During the early part of the Second World War, The Biggins housed an evacuated Moorland School from Blackburn and was destroyed by fire in 1942.

Rigmaden estate evolved from a house built by Thomas Godsalve in around 1680. The last of his descendants sold the estate to the Satterthwaite family of Lancaster, from whom in 1823 the estate was purchased by Christopher Wilson, of Abbot Hall, Kendal, partner in a local bank. Thomas Godsalve's little home was demolished and much of the stonework incorporated in a new hall. Extra land was purchased, boosting the acreage of the estate to over 9,400. Christopher left Rigmaden to his son, William, and it then passed to Christopher Wyndham Wilson, known (but not always to his face) as Kit. An exceptional man, standing almost six feet and wearing an imposing beard, Kit was High Sheriff of Westmorland in 1884 and served as a colonel in the Westmorland and Cumberland Yeomanry. In 1885 he arranged for the Lune to be bridged, providing a link between the two parts of his estate and the railway station at Barbon. To use the bridge, one had to acquire a key to the locked gates from the benefactor. Fifty such keys were issued to family, friends, parson and doctor. Public access to the bridge was permitted from the late 1920s through the good offices of C. Hulme Wilson.

Kit's farming activities began in 1880. He kept the standard breeds, of course, but also transformed local farming by extending the number of different animals. Instead of moaning about a wet haytime he conserved a substantial amount of winter forage, in which matter he was half a century ahead of his time. Visiting Holland, he was impressed by the black-and-white Friesian type of cow, which he subsequently introduced to the upper Lune (where it is today the commonest breed of cattle). He also kept a flock of Suffolk sheep. Farming occupied his restless mind for about four years. He also inherited a deer park, a square mile of land flanked by iron railings, lying to the west of the road from Kirkby Lonsdale. The height of the railings could be increased to around 7 feet 6 inches. Here, in the 1870s, the several species of deer included wapiti from North America, and sika, which evolved on the islands of the Japanese archipelago and thrived when introduced into English parks. Sika that escaped from Rigmaden in the later years of the park found cover and abundant food in Roeburndale, off Lunesdale.

The master of Rigmaden was sometimes seen strolling along the streets in Kirkby Lonsdale with a pet badger or otter on a lead. His pet monkey cavorted on the roof of Rigmaden. He was the subject of fanciful tales and was said to have bought an elephant which his wife would not allow him to bring home. Another story concerned a pheasant which he fired at as it flew over the house; the dead bird fell into the larder!

The Rigmaden stud was founded on the introduction of a selection of high-class fell pony mares to the hackney stallion 'Sir George'. The fillies from this cross were put to their sire and in-breeding was repeated for another generation. The height of a Wilson pony was kept well down (under 14 hands) but the bone quality and action made it popular from the first. The ponies were usually bay in colour. Five Wilson ponies were sold at Norfolk in September 1895 for an average of 700 guineas each. 'Sir George' won the annual show of the Royal Agricultural Society of England on eight occasions. A famous mare, 'Snorer', was born with a film covering one of her nostrils. The groom cut the film but shreds remained and gave rise to the snoring sound when the pony moved briskly. 'Snorer' ii, iii, iv and v all followed. Rigmaden Park had a riding school, a grand name for a roofed-in yard, associated with which were 14 tie stalls and several loose boxes.

The Wilsons were keen supporters of the Otter Hounds. Ironically, otters are now being coaxed back into the river. Charles, Kit's brother, was also a sporting man. He lived at Oxenholme and founded a pack of staghounds, serving as Master for half a century. The quarry was red deer, emparked until required for hunting and, hopefully, restored to the park at the end of the day. One stag became so familiar with the terrain it made directly for an island of shingle in the Lune, the water breaking its scent and cheating the hounds. The staghounds were disbanded after the Second World War and descendants of the red deer are found today on the fells to the east of Lunesdale, from which they venture down to graze in the fields in the vale.

Kit Wilson had the first car in Westmorland (registration number EC 1). When electricity was installed at Rigmaden in 1883, it was the third country house in England to have an electrical supply. Kit founded a trout hatchery, rearing both rainbow and brown trout. Lunesdale trout, entrained, appeared on the breakfast tables of the wealthy in London. The two tarns in which fish were reared took their names – Kitmere and Wyndhammere – from the owner's name. Rigmaden was occupied by evacuees during the Second World War, but William Wilson, great grandson of Kit, restored the main part of Rigmaden Park to its original state and members of the Wilson family still occupy the estate.

73 *Rigmaden, with iron gates and railings.*

Jonty Wilson, the blacksmith of Kirkby Lonsdale, knew the Wilson family well and was fond of recalling the servants' balls held at Rigmaden each Christmas. Guests became unsteady on their feet one year when a groom served home-made wheat wine. Christopher was an old man by the time the First World War brought dramatic changes to the social life of the country. One of his sons, Leonard, was a captain in the Army, and came home on leave with some young officers asking if a party might be held. Christopher insisted that celebrations should be delayed until the signing of the Armistice so a spoof telegram was sent to Rigmaden Park from Kirkby Lonsdale proclaiming the end of the war. The party was held, but when Christopher discovered he had been deceived the balloon went up – and out came the hunting crop.

Leck Hall, the home of Lord Shuttleworth, lies between the village and Ireby and evolved from High House. The estate was developed from 1771 onwards by the Welch family. In 1952 they sold it to the Kay-Shuttleworth family of Gawthorpe Hall, near Burnley, who also owned the Barbon estate and Barbon Manor. Lord Shuttleworth, a Liberal MP, was known to deal fairly with his servants. Wulstan Atkins, son of Sir Ivor Atkins and godson of the composer Edward Elgar, remembered visits to the Leck Hall estate, which was then owned by Henry Welch. He first came up as a child in about 1909 and his family visited Leck every January. The association between the Atkins and Welch families developed through a friendship at Cheltenham Ladies College between Wulstan's mother and Mary, the wife of Henry. He was a barrister who never practised and a keen organist who spent a good deal of his own money installing a fine organ in the local church, which stood several miles from his home. He would visit the church to practise on Friday evening. The blower was activated by a small electric motor. One evening the engine mis-fired and the organist was dashed against some obstacle and died.

Barbon Manor, perched high above the entrance to Barbondale, was built as a Victorian retreat in a forested situation. The house was designed by E.M. Barry for Sir James Kay-Shuttleworth and constructed in 1863 in a French Classical style. As a stately home it seems small, because the tower and west wing were demolished in 1955. What remained was remodelled by Claude Phillimore. The Shuttleworth family has been associated with this area since 1591, when the manor of Barbon was purchased. An annual car and motor-cycle rally takes place locally courtesy of the owner of Barbon Manor.

Lunefield, at Kirkby Lonsdale, belonged to the Harris family but in 1899 was sold to the widowed Countess of Bective at Underley. She died in 1928, when Lunefield became the property of the Co-operative Holiday Association. During the Second World War it was requisitioned by the military but then resumed its role as a holiday centre until the late 1950s. Badly affected by dry rot, it was demolished in 1959. The site, not far from the town centre, is now occupied by housing.

At Hornby, in the lower part of Lune Valley, the dominant building is a fine castle. Local historian Dr A.J. White notes that all that remains of a medieval castle is the great tower. Parts of the older Hornby Castle were swept away in the early 18th century by new owner Colonel Charteris. In 1720 he built a plain Georgian range across the front of the old tower which was remodelled in the late 1840s by Pudsey Dawson and in the 1880s by the Foster family to create a Gothic appearance. When Sir Harold Parkinson acquired the Castle in 1939 he reduced the living accommodation to more manageable proportions by removing the roof from certain parts.

Entries from the diary of George Smith, estate manager at Hornby from January 1819 to December 1826, have been compiled by modern historian Phil Hudson and given an astonishing insight into daily life at this celebrated Lunesdale estate (apart, that is, from the manager's unscrupulous activities). The state of local coal pits was a major topic, a new shaft having been measured by one Thomas Bowskill for a pit at Tatham. The manager settled with him for a share of Smearhaw Colliery for 1817 and 1818. William Holmes called with two greyhounds and coursed in the Priories, when Mr Whaley was also present with his greyhound, which killed four hares. Richard Raynes Broomfield paid for his wool tithe, and Richard Skirrow paid for his tithe of wool, lamb and calf for 1818. The estate manager was at Lancaster on Candlemas Saturday, 20 February. Wm. Mashiter called and paid a half year's rent for his farm called Higher Snab. Christopher Harrison came with a horse and cart from Heysham and took some willow boughs back to plant. Mr Wallace and the manager measured the masonry work of the two cottages [later Becketts] in Hornby and of the pig cotes and crossyard wall to the stable at the Launds House.

The manager attended a Vestry meeting in Hornby Chapel at which wardens were nominated and chosen. The estimated expenses of the chapelry for the year ending Easter 1819 were £45. Hornby Manor Court was held at the Castle on April 22 and on the following day Tatham Manor Court assembled at Hall Barns. Rent day was 26 April at Hornby Castle, when the manager dined with the tenants at the Castle Hill. On 17 May the manager was at Tatham Pit in the morning and shooting rooks at Snab in the afternoon. The drainers of the Bentham Moor Allotment called on the morning of 24 June. On 14 July Thomas Blezard fetched 20 Scotch Cows from beyond Gearstones [near Ribblehead]. They had been purchased by John Whaley for Mr Wright at Askrigg Fair in Wensleydale.

Chapter 6

Farming Topics

The farmsteads in the upper Lune Valley today are of stone and slate. Early dwellings had high-pitched gables and were thatched. Dwellings made of stone were constructed from the mid-17th century and invariably, above the front door, was a stone inscribed with the initials of the man and women responsible for its construction. A central passage divided the farmhouse into two parts. In the Sedbergh area there might be a wooden gallery for spinning and handloom weaving.

Among the best documented farms in the upper dale is Middleton Hall, just south of Sedbergh, a fortified manor house which today presides over a 750 acre farm that carries dairy cattle, plus followers, store cattle and a large flock of breeding sheep. Thomas de Middleton built himself a hall and pele tower at Middleton in the middle of the 14th century. The tower has disappeared but the medieval hall still stands, together with its fine windows and two-centred arched doorways. In the 15th century the house was strengthened by an 18ft curtain wall, a gatehouse, a corner tower and a crenellated parapet.

The house remained in Middleton hands until the 17th century, the family holding their lands in Lunesdale by the annual rendering of a cast of falcons to the lord of Kendal. The Middletons were unable to maintain a male succession and are gone, but not forgotten. Above the doorway of Middleton Hall is an inscription: *Venturum exhoresco them* (I dread the coming day). The building came up for sale after the Civil War, since when there have been many owners. The present tenants, the Watson family, carry on the farming tradition, the home fields being green and verdant while up on the fell sheep compete at the grazings with red deer descendants of the deer once hunted in the Lune Valley for sport.

F.W. Garnett, in *Westmorland Agriculture 1800-1900*, described the transformation of the commons into a tidy and more productive landscape

74 *Old-time Market Day, Kirkby Lonsdale.*

of hedges and walls. Drystone walls are strikingly evident in the topmost reaches of Lunesdale. The commons had been capable only of half-starving the animals pastured upon them until paring and burning, fencing and draining, liming, ploughing and sowing transformed the landscape and

increased the annual rental from between 6d. and 1s. per acre to 20s. to 30s. per acre. Stone was the handiest material for building and maintaining boundaries, and walls were built with mutual help to a standard height of 4 feet 6 inches. When skilled wallers were employed, they were paid up to threepence an hour.

75 *Shepherd and the Howgill Fells (by Edward Jeffrey).*

The wall, constructed without a dab of mortar, was in fact two walls resting side by side on large 'footing' stones and held together by big stones known as 'throughs'. Small stones were carefully packed into spaces left between the two sections of the wall. The whole was capped by 'cam' stones which sloped at an angle of 45 degrees, protecting the wall by 'turning the weather'. The great period of walling was the time of the Enclosure Awards. So remote from habitations were some of the walls, the builders probably camped near their work for days on end. A waller did not like to move his material far, so walls are a guide to local geology. Large pieces of stone or slate were transported by horse-drawn sled, the stones being broken on site into convenient sizes. In 1845 a rood of wall cost eight shillings, the price including the cost of gathering and carting.

F.W. Garnett introduced us to a typical farm labourer of the 19th century: 'Till I was wedded I had wrought for my father, and had got clothes when I wanted them. We had always a few sheepskins for breeches, and used to spin during winter nights. As to money, I never thought anything about it. When I got married, we had just seven shillings between us, when all was over.' The labourer had taken over an empty cottage with some peat moss and a garden for half a guinea. His parents provided the furniture. He was paid 6d. a day and his keep, which was augmented by what his wife might earn from spinning. Yet the labourer felt well satisfied. About a century later, in 1909, farm wages were paid half yearly, a top man receiving from £18 to £20, a woman £12 to £14, and a boy £5 to £9. Included in the wages were board, lodging and washing. A farmer needing help went to the Whitsun and Martinmas hiring fairs. He was usually looking for a sturdy lad and for a girl to help his wife. After the First World War many of the hired lads were 'townies', notably from Barrow-in-Furness. The removal from a terraced house in Barrow to a fellside farm flanked by high hills must have been traumatic. What sort of lodging conditions and food he might expect was a matter of chance, only local people knowing which farm was a 'starvation place'.

At most farms life was tolerable, and the lads were welcomed and soon made part of the family. The food was substantial, with poddish (porridge), ham and eggs and home-made bread for breakfast. Cheese and bread were available for elevenses. At dinnertime, meat was carved by the farmer, there were abundant vegetables, and a pudding course would follow. Farm tea was early, and in summer was usually eaten out-of-doors, and consisted of a basket of home-made bread, home-made jam, slabs of fruit cake or gingerbread and, quite often, a plate of pasty. Supper would be served at about six o'clock.

Jonty Wilson's father, Robert Gilgrass Wilson, was employed in the running of the Home Farm for the Paget-Tomlinsons. For his work he was paid 22s. a week, which was 2s. more than the wage of an ordinary labourer but scarcely enough for his family of ten children. Mother told Jonty in later life that the expenditure on food per head, each day, could not exceed 1¾d. or they would be in debt. A Lunesdale butcher, William Middlesbrough, was kept busy during the season slaughtering pigs. He would set off on a pony with his equipment and the pig mortality rate was about five a

76 *Sheepdogs at a Trial.*

77 *The indispensable sheepdog.*

day. He charged half a crown per pig and if the farmer wished him to return next day to work on the carcase an extra shilling or so was demanded.

John Garnett Carr, born at Hutton Roof in 1885, was a farmer's son who worked as a lad on the land. He recalled men mowing corn with scythes which had bows put on them so the corn would lay straight. Women helped collect the corn into sheaves and tied band round them. Thrashing took place with flails. Young men liked to use the flail in winter because it meant working in a warm barn, the corn being laid on a springy wooden floor. When John stayed at his grandfather's farm near Kirkby Lonsdale, he helped thrash 16 acres of corn (in four large sacks) with a flail. The first machine that came to the district was a portable one brought to the farm by horse power. Carr recalled meadow grass being scythed with a blade five feet six inches long. A 'new edge' was put on the scythe using a strickle, a square wooden object pricked with holes that was normally attached to the scythe blade and contributed towards the implement's balance. You rubbed a piece of real bacon fat on the strickle, then sprinkled sand on top. This worked into the holes and gave the strickle an abrasive surface.

John Carr's brother once ploughed six acres at Lupton with a horse-drawn plough in five days. The Clydesdale and Shire breeds of horse were masters of the dusty roads, although at Kirkby Lonsdale there was a better class of horse. Many of these were 'throw-outs' from the celebrated Rigmaden stables but were, nonetheless, fine animals. Rigmaden stallions sired many a local horse, so animals in the streets of the town might be a cross with a high-class hackney. Instead of resembling the common pony – a New Forest, Dales or Fell pony – they had 'a good bit of action'.

Fashion in cattle type has changed noticeably over the years. Longhorn cattle were supplanted by Shorthorn, which in turn were displaced by the Friesian cattle. In 1935 the Shorthorn was in the numerical ascendancy, with

19,908 licensed bulls. The Friesian, introduced from the Low Counties, could muster only 1,219. The Shorthorn name is confusing. Before the fashion for de-horning cattle when young developed, this breed had quite long horns, but the name distinguished them from the breed known as the Longhorn. The rise of the Shorthorn was rapid and for a century and more it was *the* cow of the dale country, both tough and thrifty. Its milk was rich in butterfat and useful for making butter and cheese. 'Beastings', the custard-like first flush of milk produced by a calving cow, were made into an appetising pudding. Subsequent milk was fed to the calves three times a day. In due course a calf's diet would consist of skimmed milk and linseed. Hill farmers with Shorthorn stocks worked hard and long for little return, and in the slump early in the last century good cows sold for well below £20. Prices soared in the war, but by the 1930s slump conditions had returned. The demand for more milk continued, however, so some outside blood – the Ayrshire breed – was introduced to increase the yield. The farmer got more milk but 'lost the carcase'.

A government register of dairy cattle in the 1930s revealed that the Friesian was the highest milk producer, the first five beasts on the register being of this type. Yet the Shorthorn was still common. Enthusiasts for the old type of Shorthorn met at Penrith in January 1944, and formed the Northern

78 *Hill sheep: the Rough Fell breed is in the foreground; the Swaledale breed has the grey muzzle.*

79 *Head of a Rough Fell tup.*

Dairy Shorthorn Society. Six years later, the herd book having been closed, no outside blood could be introduced. The purity of the Dales Shorthorn was assured at a time when the black-and-white Friesian was moving in.

The fells have been grazed by sheep for centuries. Counting sheep in the old style hints at the shared Celtic heritage of hill farmers in the county of Cumbria and Wales, a popular variant of the sheep-counting numerals from one to ten running: yan, tyan, tedera, meddera, pimp; sethera, lethera, hovera, dovera, dick. A Welsh farmer counting sheep might notch a piece of wood for units of five. The Crag Sheep of Farleton were usurped by the Dales-bred breed and Teeswaters by blue-faced Wensleydales. Fell sheep were clipped later than lowland sheep because the wool did not 'rise' as soon. Farmers on the slaty Howgills developed their own breed, the Rough Fell, which underpinned Kendal's wool trade at a time when the grey town's motto was 'wool is my bread'. The only guide we have to the breed's origins is an observation of George Culley in 1794. The sheep has spiral horns, black face and black legs, and its eyes are fierce and wild-looking. Culley noted 'a short, firm carcass ... covered with long, open, coarse wool; the fleeces weighed from 3½ to 4 lbs each and sold in 1792 for 6d. a lb'.

80 *Just beyond this drystone wall at Newbiggin-on-Lune is St Helen's Well, claimed by some to be the source of the river.*

Lowe (1842), supporting the notion that Rough Fell sheep had their origin in Cumberland and Westmorland, observed that, travelling north, they became the foundation of the Scotch Blackfaced breed.

During the past century, the Blackfaced Heath or Muir sheep had been gradually improved, its development proceeding along different lines and resulting in three distinct varieties evolving in the county, viz Scotch, Rough Fell and Swaledale. Garnett, in his *Westmorland Agriculture 1800-1900*, supposed that the sheep of the county were descended from the Blackfaced Heath sheep. Lowe commented that by crossing with Herdwicks in the west, Cheviots in the north and the Crag Sheep of the south, different types were evolved. Even then, these were unique to their particular districts: 'Some of them have a large portion of white in their face and legs; some have these parts speckled and others, totally black; they are, in general, horned, high-shouldered, narrow backed, flat sided, strong boned, and many with thick, rough, hairy legs. The wool is coarse and long.'

Although the Rough Fell breed had been pure for many generations it was not until 1927 that a Breed Association was formed and a Flock Book instituted to ensure reliable pedigree recording. The area covered by the Association embraced a large part of the fell land in the county of Westmorland and part of the West Riding of Yorkshire. At the first meeting, held at the YMCA Room at Kendal, Joseph Ward of Cooper House, Selside was unanimously appointed chairman. The president for many years was

81 *Fine example of drystone walling.*

Sir S.H. Scott of The Yews, Windermere; he retired in 1951. The aims of the Association were to spread the breed and capture the export trade. Twenty-four registered Rough Fell rams were exported to the Isle of Man for crossing with Swaledales. Rough Fell ewes proved excellent mothers and were in great demand for the breeding of the notable Westmorland Half-bred.

Hugh Handley, who farmed Park House, Ravenstonedale for 64 years, and retired to a cottage in the village in 1957, was a mine of information about Rough Fell sheep. When he was a boy, a good Rough Fell ram might bring £5. He considered the breed much improved during the past half century. They were cleaner, more uniform and not quite as hard in the wool, though 'they could still do with being a bit softer in the cut than they are!' Compared with the Swaledale breed, the Rough Fell dressed a heavier carcase and clipped a great weight of wool. Mr Handley ran his thousand-strong flock on Green Bell where the bottom land had been improved by being mechanically drained using the Cuthbertson plough. Sheep numbers almost doubled at the end of March and the beginning of April with the arrival of the lambs. As many as nine dogs kept the sheep under control at gathering time, and the farmer usually bought them ready trained at a cost ranging from £10 to £30. He drove flocks to market at Kendal, 19 miles away, taking two days over the journey. The ewes stood up well to the rigours of the route.

Early in October, when there was a special sheep sale at Kendal, over thirty wagons containing sheep would leave the local railway station at 4 a.m. so that the stock was in time for market. As in the Lake District, there was a Shepherds' Meet twice a year, just after clipping time, when stray, unclipped sheep were sorted out, and in autumn, after dipping, when strays were returned to their rightful owners. In the summer of 1980, the Wilson family of Low Borrow Bridge and two other holdings adjacent to the Howgill Fells had a total acreage approaching 1,000, with rather more sheep than acres. At that time,

82 *Drystone wall showing the capstones.*

farmers with stray sheep taken up during gatherings in July and November attended a Shepherds' Meet at Tebay, with the object of returning the strays to their rightful owners as indicated by distinctive sheep marks. The Meet was subsequently held at Langdale, some four miles away.

Sheep-stealers were once hanged at Gibbet Hill, near the Fair Mile, which traverses the lower western flank of the Fells. A Tup Fair was held at Orton on the second Friday in October. Carts laden with tups set out from the fell districts on the previous day, and black-faced rams might be purchased for 15s. each. Gin was the favourite tipple of the livestock dealers at the local market; who sealed their deals with it. A farmer who secured numerous bargains was apt to become 'market proud', the liquor having gone to his head. Zig-zagging home with horse and trap, he was a danger to other road users.

Rough Fell sheep – the Kendal Roughs – have been associated with Middleton Hall for centuries. The mark of the flock is a red 'pop' on the 'hook'. Gimmer sheep have the tips of their ears clipped, a custom going back to Norse times, when it was a lug (or law) mark. Clipping sheep at Middleton Hall is still a protracted affair, but in early July 1879 there was a special event known as T'Middleton Ha' Clippin'. The tenant at Middleton was W. Bowness. He was about to retire from farming and clearly did not want his neighbours and friends to forget him. The Clipping was the culmination of a tradition begun by his father seventy years before. Two thousand sheep were clipped and 1,000 lambs had their tails docked and were dipped. A

83 *A Dales sheepdog.*

representative of the *Lancaster Guardian* noted that gathering stock from the fell was a job undertaken by 13 men, each with his dog.

Dawn broke on a dull day, with a hint of rain. Happily by 6 a.m., when the vast flock had been driven down to the Hall, conditions were brighter. The work could not be carried out when the wool was damp. In the courtyard the sheep were 'folded', or kept in batches, and 70 'creels', or large, four-legged stools, arranged for the clippers. Almost a hundred clippers were involved, but the workforce varied in size as men came and went. It took five hours to clip and pack away the fleeces, as well as mark the sheep to identify them with the farm. The clippers attended to the ewes and then the young male sheep, or wethers. The *Lancaster Guardian* noted that 'the noise or click of such a number of shears produced a noise similar to that of some hundreds of guests at a dinner table with their knives and their forks. Men were marking sheep at the rate of between 416 and 528 animals per hour.'

84 *Draining by hand on a farm near Leck.*

85 *Fred Taylor, cheesemaker, who began his working life at the Creamery in Dentdale.*

As a sheep was divested of its wool, other sheep were dragged to the shearer by one of the attendant boys. The loss of the wool also removed traces of the distinctive mark of the Middleton Hall flock so sheep were re-marked by Messrs Metcalfe, Brown and Hardacre. 'A number of neatly-dressed farmers' daughters walked to and fro amongst the workers and lookers-on, supplying them without stint with bread, cheese, sandwiches, tea, beer, &c.' In the 'fleecing-room' adjoining the courtyard fleeces were folded and stored by a team of people with 'busy hands and cheerful tongues'. Several men wearing waterproof leggings and a breast apron worked in an out barn. They 'shirled', or docked, the tails of 1,000 lambs. The animals were subsequently plunged into a tub of sheep-dip, then kept for a time in

86 *Approach to Middleton Hall.*

a special box to drip-dry: 'Four men were employed in *shirling* the lambs'
tails, two or three men in handing the lambs backwards and forwards, one
in preparing the dip and three in dipping. Two men took hold of the legs of a
lamb, one by its fore and the other by its hind legs, while the third held the
head, so that dip did not reach the eyes.'

The work done, about 350 people, sixty at a time, sat down to dinner
in the dining room. Forty or fifty young ladies, 'all tidily dressed for work',
distributed refreshments under the direction of Miss Deborah Smith, the
housekeeper. She had prepared two rounds of boiled beef, weighing 110 lb,
a flank of roasted beef (90 lb), three quarters of veal (96 lb), a ham, 30 rice

87   *A shepherdess, Middleton Hall.*

88 *Courtyard of Middleton Hall.*

89 *Middleton Hall.*

puddings, 10 veal pies, 238 lb of new potatoes, 'besides pea puddings, gooseberry pies and sundry other edibles'. More food and drink was served, and then the Middleton Hall Sports began, attended by Lady Bective. A horse-trotting match, from the Hall gate to the *Swan Inn* and back, was won by 'Fanny', a brown trotter owned by Mr J. Clark, who claimed 25s. in prize money. Athletic events followed, including Cumberland and Westmorland-style wrestling, for monetary prizes. The spacious dining hall of the house being too small for the numbers of people attending, dancing took place in the courtyard, the young folk continuing until 'far into the next morning'.

Thanks and good wishes were extended to Mr Bowness, the farmer who was giving up Middleton Hall farm in favour of one of

90 *Old and new at Middleton Hall.*

91 *Swaledale sheep on the flanks of Wild Boar Fell.*

92a & 92b *Fell ponies.*

93 *Remote farm-house at Leck.*

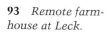

Topstones

Tracers

Headstones

Footings

94 *Details of a wallhead on a dry-stone wall.*

95 *Sheep gathering.*

96 *Gathering bracken for stock bedding.*

his nephews. The newspaper correspondent ended his story by mentioning
Mr Bowness' retirement 'from an active pastoral life with the good name
of his neighbours, a sincere wish that his last years may be spent in peace
and quiet, and that he may be gathered to his fathers in a ripe old age'. The
Middleton Ha' Clippin' was to be recorded in verse by John Collinson, who
attended the event in late June 1903, and wrote:

> Come gither up yer farmers!
> This lang breet summer's day
> An' gae wi' ma a-clippin'
> Ere we ma' [mow] the meadow hay.

The Lunesdale Agricultural Association, formed in 1839, had an unsettled
existence until 1897, when Lord and Lady Henry Bentinck allowed it to occupy
a site in the grand setting of Underley Park. Jonty Wilson remembers old-
time farming operations – hand-work – including men threshing grain on the
barn floor with flails. In a district of varying types of soil, farming was mixed,
some holdings growing acceptable corn, others keeping milk cattle. Jonty
Wilson watched a sower distributing seed with his hands and remembers
seeing a row of men with scythes moving across a field, mowing the corn.
His father told him that if a scythe was set correctly it should whistle as it
cut through the vegetation. (A plough that was 'turning right' was said to
murmur). At harvest time, the scythemen were followed by children who
picked up pieces of straw and twisted them into bands. Women gathering the
corn used the bands to tie up the sheaves. Later those sheaves were put up

97 *Jonty Wilson.*

98 *Hand-clipping sheep at a Cumbrian farm, 1967.*

into stooks – eight sheaves at a time – propped up against each other in such a way that the grain was exposed to a drying wind and sunshine.

At Kirkby Lonsdale, on market day, country families arrived with produce for sale. Main Street and Market Street were occupied by farmers' carts which were propped on trestles when the horses were removed. Displayed in the carts were fowls, butter, eggs, potatoes, turnips and other choice rural edibles. The Market Square was set out with hurdles for sheep, the Swinemarket was visited by anyone wishing to deal in pigs, and cattle were on view up Fairbank. Horses for sale stood in a field opposite the post office. Upper Lunesdale was well populated by locally born people until the 1930s, many being employed on a farm that today would be operated by a man and his son assisted by machines.

99 *Westmorland-type porch on Pool House, Lowgill.*

Chapter 7

From Drovers and Packmen
to the Railway Age

In autumn, before the railways, thousands of cattle intended for the English marts passed down Lunesdale to grazing areas where they might regain their condition before setting off on another stage of their journey. At Mansergh a hostelry called the *Durham Ox* stood beside what was known as the 'Scotch Road'. Mireside, a stone structure with a slate roof, was once a smithy where eight men attended to local horses. Driven cattle might need their feet reinforced against the rough terrain. Such cattle were 'thrown', or turned on their backs, and light shoes were fitted. Only the outside claw was shod using a fairly light iron, rarely more than one sixteenth of an inch thick. The shoe extended up the inside of the claw and was secured by three nails.

For centuries goods were moved from place to place by packhorse train. Jonty Wilson, the blacksmith at Kirkby Lonsdale, had a grandfather in the trade who was born in 1834 and died at the age of 89. As the owner of packhorses, he accompanied trains of them along the green tracks of the north. Jonty referred to their use by the drovers – 100,000 head of cattle, with flocks of other beasts, making an annual pilgrimage. They were also, of course, the route of the packhorse man, the yeoman and the humble pedlar. Packhorse men were described by Jonty as small, independent businessmen. Their dress was distinctive, a coat of hodden grey, knee breeches and gartered woollen stockings. The headgear was a low-crowned beaver hat (actually rabbit skin) which was made at Masongill, the tucked-away hamlet near Ingleton. According to Jonty, the packhorse men kept clear of the drovers, having their own places of call. They were inclined to sleep rough and ate frugally, carrying a bag of oatmeal (in a *haver*sack), onions and cheese.

The tinkling of a brass bell worn by the leading horse heralded the approach of a packhorse train. The favourite animal was the Dales cob, which was somewhat larger than the ubiquitous Fell pony. Packhorse animals were

100 *Cattle droving (by Celia King).*

joined together, the tail of one being plaited to form a ring through which was passed a rope that extended from the halter of the animal next in line. The panniers were usually made of wood and connected by hinge to a bow of metal extending over the back of the animal. Another hinge was fitted at the point where the ledge jutted out from a pannier. Turf might be used to pad the animal's back, one disadvantage of the split-load being its liability to move and make the animal sore. The loads were various. Salt was in regular demand, much of the meat consumed by local folk in winter being salted down to preserve it. Salt might be bartered against the products of the dales such as wool, cheese and butter.

The Galloway Gate was a busy route that entered Westmorland at Eamont Bridge, at the outflow of Ullswater, and took a southward course to Kirkby Lonsdale. K.J. Bonser, who researched the droving trade, found an early reference to the road in a charter of 1186-1201, whereby 'Gilbert son of Fitz-Raynfray gave to William de Arundel for his service all the land between Galwaithegate and Lon.' William Farrer, in *Records Relating to the Barony of Kendale*, was interested in the reference to Galwaithegate, which he described as 'this curious lane, running as directly north and south as the hills and dales permit'. The route had been used for centuries since the date of the aforementioned charter 'as a driving road for cattle from Scotland to England, and was probably used by the Scotch for their longer expeditions into England in the time of King Stephen and Edward II. When sheep, cattle or ponies were being driven south from Shap the stages were short and the resting places frequent. Between Tebay and Kirkby Lonsdale they were Low Borrow Bridge, Lambrigg Park, Three Mile House and Old Town, stages of 5 to 6 miles a day.' Jonty Wilson

101 *The pack pony (by Godfrey Wilson).*

said the Galloway Gate began to lose its importance after about 1860, when railways were becoming established.

An inn, now a farm known as Mansergh High, has a representation of a packhorse in relief above the main door and was clearly once of droving significance. The farm stands at an elevation of 500 feet. Lower down the hill is a barn which was once fitted with a bell that possibly signalled the approach of packhorses to a depot on Barbon Fell. Beckfoot bridge, which spans Barbon Beck, a tributary of the Lune, in a single graceful arch, is a mere two feet wide with low parapets and is the best surviving example of a packhorse-type bridge in the district. It is believed to have been constructed in 1571 by John Hardy of Barbon at a cost of 22s. 4d. Low parapets were necessary to provide clearance to packhorse loads. If the beck were in flood, cattle would be urged across the bridge.

When each parish seemed to live for itself, the Hayhursts had a mill at Selleth. They were often visited by Jonty Wilson who occasionally led a loaded packhorse from mill to customer. Robert Hayhurst, the miller, cautioned him to let the men at the farm lift off the sacks and be sure to lead, rather than ride, the horse on the return journey. Jonty contrived to ride to within a few hundred yards of the mill before dismounting.

A celebrated feature of the Lune Valley is the Devil's Bridge at Kirkby Lonsdale. For centuries, until a new bridge downriver was opened in 1932,

102 *Packhorse bridge at Beckfoot, on a tributary of the Lune.*

Devil's Bridge was the principal entry to the town. The old structure, which is still sound and is a major tourist attraction, has spanned a limestone gorge since medieval times and there is some mystery about its true age. It may be that the first attempt to bridge the gap was a structure made of wood. A stone bridge was in need of repair in the 13th century, when a grant of pontage was made for this purpose. Three graceful arches spring from stone piers and a squat column of stone, set in a recess, is inscribed 'Fear God, Honour the King, 1633'. There is also an oft-repeated story of how an old lady duped the Devil. When no bridge existed she found herself on one bank of the river and her cow on the other. Wading across would be dangerous so the Devil offered to build a bridge overnight, so the lady could recover the cow, on condition that he might claim the first living thing to cross. The bridge was built and the Devil waited to claim the soul of the old lady, but she cheated him by tossing a bun across – a bun which was pursued by her little dog, which became the first living creature to cross.

John Hutton, a Kendal cleric, writing about the bridge in 1780, referred to a hoary tale that said the Devil's Apron Strings, a cairn on Casterton Fell, was formed of stones dropped by Satan during his bridge-building episode. It was implied locally that, had he not accidentally dropped this load, the bridge would have been wider. Downriver, marking the old Westmorland/Lancashire boundary, is a block of limestone with a hole through it. Inevitably, because of its strange appearance, it has been demonised as the Devil's Neck Collar.

103 *Jonty Wilson with a fell pony.*

The bridge was closed to traffic when a new road bridge opened in 1932 and is now a tourist hotspot, with parking facilities, a snack bar and, at weekends, an impressively large number of parked motor-cycles. The fact that the comparatively narrow bridge accommodated all the traffic before 1932 is remarkable. Several traffic accidents were the subject of a coroner's inquest. In 1851, according to the 3 May issue of the *Westmorland Gazette,* the omnibus operating between Kirkby Lonsdale and the railway station at Hornby came to grief. As the vehicle returned from Hornby between nine and ten o'clock on Sunday night, it was driven on to the bridge at a moderate speed, passing the middle of the bridge and descending the western incline with increased velocity. The right-hand fore wheel struck the last kerbstone at the base of the parapet and so violent was the shock that four passengers travelling outside, besides the driver, were precipitated forward, some landing amongst the horses and others against the wall.

Mr John Morphet, the driver, 'to whom the melancholy occurrence proved fatal', was supposed in the first instance to have been dashed against the wall, head foremost, an opinion based on the fracture of his right temple which alone was sufficient to cause death. The luckless driver was also caught by the fore wheel, under which he was found and lingered for a while before he 'breathed his last'. Three of the passengers, Louisa Willan, William Garnett and Thomas Grundy, having extricated themselves from their perilous situation, searched for their companions and found the body of the deceased. They reported 'a profuse stream of blood flowing from his temple and life almost extinct'. A female passenger, also overlooked in the panic and 'quite bewildered with her fall and almost beside herself with fright', had run into town. Her companions on the coach panicked, thinking that she had fallen from the bridge and been 'dashed to pieces on the rocks below', and promptly alerted two surgeons, Messrs Batty and James. No imputation of negligence on the part of the deceased was recorded, and the newspaper account noted that 'the melancholy occurrence was the result of mere accident which, considering the intense darkness of the night, the ponderous size of the omnibus and the exceeding narrowness of the bridge, may be reasonably accounted for without throwing the blame of neglect on the unhappy sufferer'. At the inquest, a verdict of 'accidental death' was returned.

The new bridge was named Stanley Bridge after the Right Honourable Oliver Stanley, MP for Westmorland, who officially opened it on 3 December 1932. The Devil's Bridge featured in another road accident on 29 December 1934. Again, it was night, a foggy night, and a lorry driver missed the route across the Stanley Bridge and headed towards the Devil's Bridge, crashing into a parapet. The driver escaped through a door on the passenger

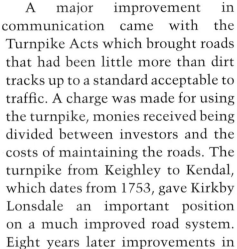

side, much to his relief. The other door, which was jammed partly open, lay above a sheer drop to the riverside rocks far below.

A major improvement in communication came with the Turnpike Acts which brought roads that had been little more than dirt tracks up to a standard acceptable to traffic. A charge was made for using the turnpike, monies received being divided between investors and the costs of maintaining the roads. The turnpike from Keighley to Kendal, which dates from 1753, gave Kirkby Lonsdale an important position on a much improved road system. Eight years later improvements in the roads from Kirkby Stephen to

104 *Packhorse sign on a farmhouse near Kirkby Lonsdale.*

105 *Old-time pedlar, Kirkby Lonsdale.*

106 *Travellers near a former toll-house at Casterton. They are heading for Appleby Fair.*

Lancaster and from Askrigg in Wensleydale to Sedbergh stimulated trade at Sedbergh, for each road passed through the town. The knitting industry prospered and mills were able to process cotton sent from Manchester as well as wool grown on the backs of local sheep.

Two documents relating to the Kirkby Lonsdale and Kendal Turnpike Road give an insight into the later days of the turnpikes. Both concern the Letting of Tolls and the Sale of a Toll Bar, and in each case the Wall Head Gate and Cow Brow Gate were involved. On 19 October 1843, Wm Romaine Gregg, Clerk to the Trustees of the Turnpike Road, and based at Kirkby Lonsdale, gave notice that the Tolls arising at the two Toll Gates would be sold by auction to the best bidder, either together or separately, at the House of Miss Roper, the *Royal Hotel*, in Kirkby Lonsdale, at 11 a.m. on 23 November. The sale would be for the term of one or three years, commencing on 1 January. The tolls were

107 *The Devil's Bridge.*

currently let at 'the clear annual rent of £438 10s.'. A Notice of Sale of the two properties is dated 1877. Mr I.E. Kilshaw would officiate at the auction, the venue of which would be the *Royal Hotel* in Kirkby Lonsdale. The first Lot was a cottage or dwelling house known as Wall Head Toll Bar with the garden and appurtenances, situate within the township of Ireby in the County Palatine of Lancaster. Lot 2 was Cow Brow Toll Bar, a cottage or dwelling house with garden and appurtenances, situate in the Township of Lupton. Cow Brow swiftly changed hands, being purchased by Edward Dodgson, who gave it to his daughter, a Mrs Baines. The property was subsequently sold to a Mr James and a Mr Tallon purchased it from him!

The coming of the railways brought an end to the packhorse era but the horse continued to have a local importance. John Wilman of the *Royal Hotel* at Kirkby Lonsdale was famed for his horses and carriages. The vehicles included Clarences, Victorias, Broughams, gigs, dog-carts, wagonettes and charabancs. Every vehicle that left the *Royal* yard was stopped just before reaching the street to be examined by Wilman as everything had to be clean and bright. Wilman had an enormous staff. A lad started by 'mucking out', or keeping the stables clean, but some workers went on to be grooms, then coachmen, at notable houses in the valley. One man was constantly employed preparing food. All the hay was chopped by machine to a length of about an inch, which rid the hay of much of its dust. The chopped hay was passed through a sort of funnel, and a quantity of oats dropped down among the chop and mixed. Coach horses were fed with some split Indian corn among other food, but horses that did slow or easy work did not benefit from such a diet.

John Wilman's special pride was a state carriage and pair (in earlier days, there were four horses, with postilions). The driver, John Teasdale, was a celebrated whip. Alexander Pearson, Undersheriff, recalled a road journey to Appleby on official duty two days before the Assize. He met the Judge, who arrived by train from London and was then borne by coach, in his scarlet robes, with Sheriff and his Chaplain in attendance, to his quarters. The coachman wore a coat fringed with gold or silver lace, knee breeches, silk stockings, silver-buckled shoes, white gloves and a three-cornered hat and white wig. Two state footmen, complete with silver-headed staves, stood on the coach's footboard. Walking on each side of the coach was the Judge's escort, tenants of the Sheriff or members of his household staff in normal life. Undersheriff Pearson walked ahead of the coach wearing his court suit or full evening dress and carrying, as did the bailiffs, wands of office. Two trumpeters sounded fanfares on silver trumpets.

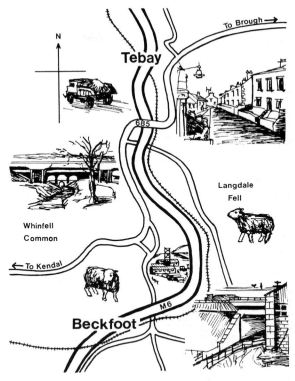

108 *Map of M6 and Lancaster-Carlisle Railway in Lune Gorge.*

Wilman allocated eight horses to a shuttle-service between Kirkby Lonsdale and Morecambe. The first coach left at 9 a.m. and a fresh pair of horses was harnessed at Morecambe for the return journey, which was of special benefit to people living in intermediate villages. A similar service operated on three days a week between Kirkby Lonsdale, Kendal and Windermere. When Kendal was reached the over-worked horses were replaced by a fresh team of four animals that travelled to Windermere or even to Ambleside. More fresh horses were waiting at the northern end of the route to ensure an immediate return. The Wilmans ended their five-times-a-day service to Kirkby Lonsdale station at the start of the Second World War. The coachman had met trains at a station situated over a mile from the town centre, collecting passengers and handling goods consigned to local tradesmen. Four horses were available to sustain a service to Arkholme station three times a day.

David Burrow of Sedbergh, the last carrier to operate between the town and Kendal, did so for 27 years. The journey took four hours. His horse, named 'Spider', drew a simple cart that had a canvas hood so goods might be kept dry when the weather was inclement. The carrier crossed the county boundary into Westmorland at Lincoln's Inn Bridge over the Lune, then faced a formidable hill road before he could relax on the long descent to Kendal. He delivered messages and shopping and collected supplies from Kendal firms for the shops of Sedbergh.

A wise old women prophesied that carriages without horses would run over Loups Fell, and in the 1840s the Lancaster and Carlisle railway stormed the heights of Shap. The company was absorbed in 1879 by the London and North Western. Tebay, a strung-out village which became a turnpike staging post in 1760, became a notable railway junction in 1861 when the main line was joined by the Stainmore Railway, later part of the North Eastern. A busy coke line, it connected North East England with industrialised Furness.

Railway engineers had long regarded the route through Ingleton and the Lune Valley as a natural means of approaching the Shap Fells and the north. George Stephenson himself considered bringing the line from Lancaster to Carlisle through Kirkby Lonsdale and Sedbergh. The project remained on the table until 1843 when it was set aside, Kendalians moving heaven and earth to assert their claim the line should pass nearer to their town. The Vale of Lune railway was also opposed by landowners who met at the *Royal Hotel*, Kirkby Lonsdale, in February 1843. Three resolutions were passed, the first stating that

> whereas the projected Railway through this district would intersect and materially injure many private grounds, cut up and destroy the most fertile portions of the valley, and mar the generally admired beauties of the Lune, and is not called for by the wants of the District, and whereas another line has been surveyed by way of Kendal, more likely to subserve the interests of commerce, for which railways are

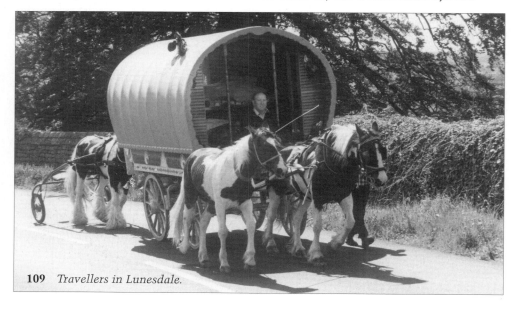

109 *Travellers in Lunesdale.*

avowedly designed, and calculated to accommodate a much larger population, it is therefore the opinion of this meeting that a decided opposition should be offered to the Line proposed by the Lune Valley.

With Railway Mania sweeping the country, advertisements in the local press in March 1845 announced the formation of the North Western Railway, intended to connect the West Riding of Yorkshire with the Lancaster and Carlisle and the west of Scotland. The Act of Parliament authorising construction of the line received the Royal Assent on 30 June 1846, and work on it began early in 1847. The formal opening between Skipton and Ingleton occurred on 26 July 1849. Bands played, cannons were fired, flags flew and a cold luncheon was enjoyed at Settle by those immediately involved. A bystander at Ingleton noticed the interest surrounding the arrival of the first load of coke, when a railway policeman (signalman) was 'looking bashful in his new livery'. The Lune Valley branch line began at Clapham, in the West Riding, and ran for seven miles in Yorkshire, then for three miles in Lancashire (to Cowan Bridge), eight in Westmorland, two more in Yorkshire (at Sedbergh), and ended with three more miles just inside the Westmorland border. The big viaduct at Ingleton initially had Midland working on one side and London and North Western on the north.

With the opening of the Settle-Carlisle line in 1876, however, the heady days were over. The route up Lunesdale from Ingleton to Lowgill settled down to a quieter existence, with four stopping trains each way. The trains operated to or from Tebay, there being no locomotive facilities at Lowgill. Life on the line quickened in 1881 when additional semi-fast trains operating

110 *Army vehicle special train, Lune Gorge.*

111 *Tebay engine shed staff at an unknown date.*

between Leeds and Penrith used the line. In 1909 the London and North Western, Midland, and Lancashire and Yorkshire companies agreed to work together, and in the following year a Lake District Express left Leeds at 10 a.m. and ran non-stop via the Ingleton branch to Penrith, connecting with a train for Keswick before continuing to Carlisle and Glasgow. The service

112 *Tebay in the days of steam.*

113   *The Manchester-Carlisle express at Tebay station.*

lasted until 1912, and was replaced by a similar Leeds-Keswick working, which was reintroduced in 1922.

Lowgill station, with attendant cottages that accommodated ten families, stood in isolation near the hamlet of Beckfoot. The railwaymen and their families survived without gas, electricity, bathrooms and water closets. Water for domestic use was piped from a spring into the back yard of the houses. They were exposed to the ravages of the Helm Wind, which raced across from the Pennines with enough force to topple anyone who was not braced against it. The winter chill prompted some of the cottagers to sleep in their overcoats. In the grim weather of March 1947 roads were jammed with snow and the railway proved indispensable for bringing in supplies. For a

114   *Barbon railway station.*

115 *Sedbergh railway station, 1928.*

time, the branch line was the only route open between England and Scotland. Two stations of special importance in Lunesdale were Kirkby Lonsdale and Barbon, the former a mile or so from the town centre. A stately home like Underley was connected by special route to the handiest station. T. Irving James, a native of Barbon, wrote in *Cumbria* magazine that the Clapham-Lowgill branch line meant mundane things like the daily newspapers, coal, farm feed stuffs, cattle, horses, farm machinery, machines for the Lunesdale Farmers' creamery and barrels of tar for the roads were all available.

The Zetland Pony Club hired a special train to convey their mounts to the annual camp in Underley Park. Special trains were also laid on at vacation periods for Casterton School. The Ingleton-Lowgill line was a useful alternative to the snow-clogged Settle-Carlisle in 1947 and 1962, but the branch was officially closed on 26 July 1966. A year later it had been stripped of its rails. Irving James was not there to see the last train but remembers the aftermath of closure, the mess of churned-up ballast 'and a long line of good, stout bridges serving no useful purpose'. The London and North Western station at Ingleton was closed to passengers on the first day of 1917 and the frontier nature of Ingleton ended with Grouping in 1923, which led to the working of the whole line, from Clapham to Lowgill, as a single unit.

The main period of growth at the junction station of Tebay was between 1880 and 1910. Old-time railwaymen reminisced about the coke traffic emanating from County Durham, five trains a day running to the steel plant of Barrow-in-Furness. A former porter recalled when goods were off-loaded from the Lancaster-Carlisle system to be put on trains using the branch line from Lowgill to Ingleton. Cans of Irish cream, each weighing 3 cwt, were re-directed to the dairy at Barbon. Railwaymen were also cowboys, able to deal with a cattle trade that operated locally. Tebay in its railway heyday provided jobs for several hundred men. The squad of porters was especially attentive when Goodwin, squire of Orton, arrived to catch the London train. He was driven to the station in a horse-drawn trap, his luggage stored in the back. On Saturdays, market trains ran to Kendal, farmers' wives with dressed fowls and baskets of butter and eggs paying a shilling fare to spend an afternoon in town and returning at about 4 p.m.

Railwaymen and their families built a new school, an Anglican church and a Methodist chapel. Gas lighting at the station turned night into day, the gas-house being linked to some of the cottages and to the local church as well. It was taken for granted that a working-class lad leaving the local school would try for a job on the railway; there was little else to do. He might

116 *Signalman at Ravenstonedale, 22 July 1961, holding the token that allows this Blackpool to South Shields holiday train to proceed from Tebay to Kirkby Stephen.*

be offered the lowly job of knocker-up, reporting at 6 p.m. and working for 12 hours, alerting 20 to 30 men an hour or so before they were due to report for duty. Or, as a 'cleaner', he would find himself on the first rung of a short ladder leading to the job of fireman, then driver. Labour being cheap, a team of eight cleaners might be set to work on one of the incoming locomotives. Four worked on each side, and before it was passed by an inspector the locomotive had to be as clean underneath as on the sides. The workers even made the footplate shine. A cleaner was issued with half a bucket of blue cleaning oil and an appropriate number of rags. One man spread the oil and his companion wiped it off.

Tebay had a large fitting shop which was the workplace of five men. Specialist jobs in the Big Shed included that of 'fire-dropper', who coaled and watered locomotives that had finished their stint, turning them on the turntable if necessary. He then knocked out the fire and cleaned the firebox and smokebox. Other workers poured coal from 10 cwt steel tubs into the tenders of locomotives that were about to go on duty. The coal was transported by train, 20 wagons at a time, from pits at Ingleton or Wigan. The 'steam-raiser' began his special task at 10 p.m. He put a hundredweight of coal in a firebox before using a long-handled spade to transfer already burning coal, from a furnace to the coal in the firebox. Railway families lived in South Terrace and Whinfell, which were built by the London and North Western, or North Terrace and Church Street, built by the North Eastern Railway.

Goods traffic heading north from Tebay had the assistance of 'bank' engines, the next five miles being gruelling, gradients as steep as 1 in 75 on the climb to Shap Summit. Help was afforded any goods train with more than 19 loose-coupled wagons, and express trains needing additional power

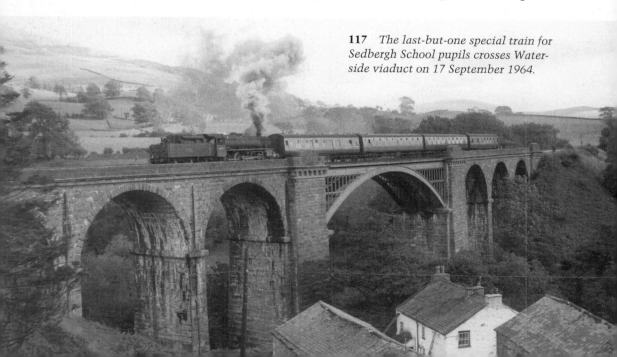

117 *The last-but-one special train for Sedbergh School pupils crosses Waterside viaduct on 17 September 1964.*

118 *The disused Waterside viaduct on the Ingleton-Lowgill railway line.*

were also assisted. As a train requiring a 'bank' engine approached Tebay, the driver of the engine sounded the whistle, known locally as 'giving a crow', and was admitted to the main line to perform his duties. Three 'bank' engines were maintained in a ready state. John Horsley worked on them for 15 years, and found the work monotonous, 'just riding up and down the hill'. Ten cwt of coal was used on the ascent. A local railwayman wrote of Tebay:

> There was an inflated idea about the power of a bank engine. It was said to be unable to travel on level track without tipping over, or backwards. The bank engine was placed on a special bit of track beside the double cottage. The duty of his fireman who lived next door was to light the fire and get up steam, while the boss cleaned the running parts and even scrubbed the blistered paintwork. Between jobs, the engine crew went home to meals and once a week with wives and market baskets crowding the cab went down to Tebay for shopping ... As business became brisker, more powerful locomotives were designed which took loads up Shap Fells without the aid of a bank engine. The cottages at the foot of the pitch were relegated to less expert workers than driver and fireman. The special little siding with crossroads for the engines was pulled up.

During the First World War, Admiralty coal from Swansea and the Midlands made a northward passage through Tebay to warships at Rosyth and the 'top' of Scotland. A Tebay man returning home told his family of some top secret equipment he had seen, the new Army vehicles known as tanks. In the Second World War, train loads of petrol were transported from depots spread along Lunesdale. The railway saga ended in July 1968 with the closure of Tebay station. The North Eastern line ceased to be used from 1962 and part of the trackbed now forms a section of the A685 road.

Being the only junction station on the Settle-Carlisle, Garsdale once had a substantial railway community, with terraced housing, a waiting room where library books were kept and Anglican services were held, and a meeting place and dance floor in the space beneath the massive water tank. A venerable and wheel-less railway carriage was dumped nearby as a refreshment room. From the Settle-Carlisle line a railway was extended into Wensleydale. Mr Bell Pratt, a Wensleydale man, went into Scotland for cattle and local farmers collected them from the station or employed a drover such as Tommy Byker of Gayle. The cattle usually arrived at Garsdale on a late train and Tommy would walk them through the night.

119 *Traffic in the Lune Gorge: M6 motorway and main Glasgow railway line.*

Chapter 8

Crafts and Industries

With a high scenic appeal and few conspicuous blemishes, the Lune Valley appears not to have been despoiled with industry and remains ripe for tourism. A traveller in the Lune Valley in the late 18th and early 19th centuries, however, would have been aware of a blend of farming with industry. The river and its many tributaries offered the textile industry a free source of water power. Almost every major settlement had its watermill or mills producing a variety of textiles, from silk to wool, and from flax (in some cases) to cotton. The decline in textile production which occurred about the mid-19th century was associated with changes in trade, both internationally and domestically. Cotton was now being imported at Liverpool and the milltowns of south-east Lancashire were in process of lusty development.

Knitting was a prime industry in the upper dale country for several centuries. In Robert Southey's novel *The Doctor*, the handknitters of Dent were described as 'terrible', meaning 'great'. Southey related how, in the 18th century, two Langdale children arrived at Dent Town to receive tuition in the local form of knitting. From the reign of the first Elizabeth, knitting as an industry fitted neatly into the economy of the dale country, being associated with sheep rearing. An ancient skill, in the 16th century it was the main domestic industry, supplementing the modest income from farming. The change from distaff to spinning wheel allowed a single spinner to provide enough yarn to keep four or five knitters busy:

> A clever lass in Dent
> Knaws how to sing and knit,
> Knaws how to carry the kit [milk pail]
> While she drives her kine to pasture.

120 *William Wilson, bobbin turner at Birks Mill, Sedbergh.*

121 *Impression of a spinning gallery (by David Hoyle).*

Adam Sedgwick, the academic born at Dent, wrote of 'little family parties, who assembled in each other's homes in turn'. A statesman's house in Dent seldom had more than two floors. The upper floor did not extend to the wall – where stood the chief fireplace – but was wainscoted off from it. Consequently, part of the ground floor near the fireplace was open to the rafters, 'which formed a wide pyramidal space, terminating in the principle chimney of the house', and it was here the family assembled, chiefly under the open rafters. To conserve fuel, there was one blazing fire, consisting of turf and logs. The gathering was known as 'goin' a sittin''. A knitting stick resembling a wooden dagger was slipped under a belt at the waist and used in conjunction with a curved needle, which slotted into a hole at the head of the stick. Many knitting sticks were made by dalesmen as presents for their sweethearts. They had romance in mind as they whittled with a knife, and nothing would impress a lady more than a finely carved knitting stick, especially if it bore the initials of the recipient. The pink-tinted stick prized by a Sedbergh lady had been fashioned from apple wood, and plum wood was valued by stick-makers. A knitting stick did not wear out but might be handed down from generation to generation. Many sticks are now treasured mementoes in dale-country houses.

122 *Dales hand knitters, from Walker's* The Costume of Yorkshire *(1814).*

The good folk of Dent knitted 'bump', or coarsely spun wool, which was delivered to them weekly. A 'bump' knitter had a peculiar swaying, bobbing movement known as 'striking the loop'. Someone might read from a classic work like *Robinson Crusoe* or *Pilgrim's Progress*. Hand-knitting was not restricted to women, men and boys knitting in between jobs, and a young Dent girl arriving home from school had to knit, say, a sleeve for a jacket before being allowed out to play. Cottage knitting was common over a wide area. Dolly Coupland sustained a knitting school at Ravenstonedale, the main output being stockings which were disposed of at Kirkby Stephen or even at Kendal. The purchasers were hosiers, who ensured the knitters had a good supply of wool to keep the trade operating. In some weeks the output of stockings at this village was a thousand pairs. Hanks of tough, undyed wool were brought into Dentdale on packhorses (later via the local carrier) and finished items – caps, mittens, gloves and stockings – were collected with the next delivery.

Sedgwick wrote of distant times when a little local wool was retained and spun into a very coarse and clumsy thread known as 'bumf'. The dalesfolk later became familiar with finer material prepared by the woolcomber. Sedgwick knew of the knitting schools, 'where the children first learnt the art many of them were to follow through life', but in 1868 he observed somewhat nostalgically that the 'sitting' was already becoming an item for the history book. 'They took their seats and then began the work of the evenings; and with a speed that cheated the eye they went on with their respective tasks. Beautiful gloves were thrown off complete; and worsted stockings made good progress ... There was no dreary deafening noise of machinery; but there was the merry heart-cheering sound of the human tongue.'

William and Mary Howitt, who arrived in Dentdale in the 1840s, watched hand knitters at work,

> rocking to and fro like so many weird wizards ... And this rocking motion is connected with a mode of knitting peculiar to the place, called 'swaving', which is difficult to describe. Ordinary knitting is performed by a variety of little motions, but this is a single uniform tossing motion of both the hands at once and the body sometimes accompanying it with a sort of sympathetic action ... They knit with crooked pins called 'pricks'; and use a knitting-sheath consisting commonly of a hollow piece of wood, as large as the sheath of a dagger, curved to the side and fixed in a belt called the cowband ... Upon the hand there is a hook, upon which the long end of the knitting is suspended that it may not dangle.

In his *Memorial by the Trustees of Cowgill Chapel*, Sedgwick regretted the loss at Dent Town of the grotesque and rude but picturesque old galleries

> which once gave a character to the streets and in some parts of them almost shut out the sight of the sky from those who travelled along the pavement. For, rude as were the galleries, they once formed a highway of communication to a dense and industrious rural population which lived on flats or single floor. And the galleries that ran before the successive doors were at all seasons places of free air; and in the summer season were places of mirth and glee and active, happy industry. For there might be heard the buzz of the spinning wheel, and the hum and the songs of those who were carrying on the labours of the day; and the merry jests and greetings sent down to those who were passing through the streets.'

Miss Elizabeth Middleton, one of the last of the Dent knitters, had old brass knitting needles she knew as 'wires' or 'pricks'. Her knitting friend, Miss Hartley, was taught to knit by her grandmother when she was aged three. In later life she donned the leather belt with a buckle used by grandmother when knitting. Her knitting stick, fashioned on a hand-lathe from ash, was a wedding gift from William Oversby, her grandfather. He and his son Edward, who were joiners, made sticks for other people. Top knitting speed was referred to as 'gallopin''. A hand knitter who did a rib of alternate knit and purl was 'nobbut canterin''. Some of the hand knitters produced stockings made of coarser material for sea-goers.

A Directory of 1838 mentioned the formerly extensive manufacture of woollen hosiery, 'which has of late years greatly declined, though some of the poor are still employed in knitting coarse stockings, etc. for miserable wages'. As an industry it finally ceased about 1880 but several local woollen mills gave the district an industrial flavour. Hebblethwaite Hall, up the Cautley Valley near Sedbergh, became a woollen mill which was operated by a Quaker named Robert Foster born in Lancaster in 1754. His schooldays were spent at Sedbergh and he went to sea at the age of 18, making three voyages to the West Indies where he was for a time a store-keeper with the family firm in Antigua. Returning to sea, he helped fight the privateers in the American War of Independence. His fighting put him at odds with the Quaker community, especially when he appeared at Brigflatts Meeting House 'with his lace cocked hat on his head and a cutlass by his side', according to Adam Sedgwick. Leaving the Navy about 1779, he became manager of his grandfather's estate at Hebblethwaite, inheriting it in 1785. He built the mill in about 1792, initially in partnership with Charles Holme, but the partnership was dissolved in 1793. In a bill posted when the estate was sold by auction in September 1812 there is mention of 'mills, and other conveniences now used in, and well adapted for, carrying on the Woollen Manufacture ...'.

Joseph Dover rented and ran the mill after 1812 and proved to be an astute businessman, increasing the level of trade. This involved spinning yarn for both cloth and knitting, the garments being transported from the mill by cart after having been put through the finishing processes. A ledger kept by John Dover mentioned various knitted goods – hose, bonts (bonnets), Du caps (Dutch caps, bonnet-like), Kilmk caps (Kilmarnock caps, as worn by children in charity schools), mitts and gloves. Hebblethwaite Mill became a bobbin and saw mill, but eventually fell into ruin, its stones being carted away for other uses. Production was moved to the larger, more convenient, Farfield Mill, which was burnt down in 1909 and rebuilt on modern lines. The sight of water cascading over broken rocks for about two hundred yards had attracted the enterprising brothers, John and James Dover, when they began to expand their woollen enterprise in about 1836, and they moved from Hebblethwaite Hall to Farfield to take advantage of a better access arrangements and water supply.

The firm of Joseph Dover and Son produced cloth when Kendal was an important woollen centre, many years before the Victorian textile boom created the mill towns of Yorkshire and Lancashire. It is presumed the cloth

123 *Mrs Elizabeth Hartley, hand knitter, Dentdale.*

124 *Knitting sticks of the finely-carved type that young men used to give their girlfriends.*

made at Farfield in its early years was from the wool of the native Rough Fell sheep. It may have been undyed, as was the 'hodden grey' of some Lakeland woollen mills. (The celebrated Lakeland huntsman, John Peel, wore a coat so 'grey', not 'gay', as in the song.) With Farfield well established, the brothers' restless natures impelled them to open two more mills nearer Sedbergh. They prospered and took over a number of local farms, part of the tenant farmer's rent then being paid in wool which was processed at the mill. It is believed that some of the yarn produced by the Dovers was knitted into gloves and stockings by the Terrible Knitters o' Dent. Four cottages at Farfield built beside a riverside lane became known as The Row and were allocated to workers, other employees living in the new hamlet of Hallbank. The millowner lived in style at Farfield House, which was built in a sunny spot.

Tom Cornthwaite, a packer in the Farfield warehouse for 32 years, began work at 6 a.m. and continued until 5.30 p.m. The firm was then making horse blankets, one of only two in England in this branch of the trade. Local wool was used, Thomas Dover attending wool sales in Lakeland and purchasing fleeces from the Herdwick breed that populated the high fells. Tom handled thick, felt-like, cloth, some of which would be used on racehorses belonging to King George V. Tradition was being maintained, blankets used on horses owned by Queen Victoria and King Edward VII having been made at Farfield: 'The Queen liked hers in quiet colours, no gaudy checks!' Some of the coarser sheetings became linings for jute horse blankets and lined collars. Black-and-red checked sheeting went to Glasgow for the railway horses, while other kinds were consigned to Australia and New Zealand, but this custom was spoilt by the introduction of the Australian Tariff.

In 1993, Bryan and Carol Hinton were weaving tweed at Farfield Mill using two Dobcross looms that were purchased on the closure of Mealbank Mill in Kendal, where they had been installed in 1936 and used until the mill closed about three decades later. The Farfield waterwheel was succeeded by a turbine, built by Gilkes of Kendal, which ceased to be used in the 1920s when electricity became available. The Hintons hailed from South Yorkshire

125 *Clara Sedgwick, hand-knitting.*

and arrived at Sedbergh as schoolteachers. Needing a change of scene, Bryan joyfully took over Pennine Tweeds at Farfield Mill from David and Gladys Douglas, who moved into town. The Hintons' new home was one of the mill cottages. Their workforce was completed by Anne Hogarth, who began working for the Douglases some twenty years before. The yarn used for weaving all-wool tweed cloth was bought in West Yorkshire, which was still the centre for the English wool industry. From the Dobcross looms came fabric for clothing and for travel rugs until 1993, when Bryan and Carol Hinton sadly decided their weaving was no longer commercially viable. They continued to sell cloth by mail order, but the looms of Farfield lapsed into silence. A woollen mill for 156 years, Farfield is now a respected Arts and Heritage Centre.

Mills proliferated in rural areas of Lancaster. Beside the swirling Lune at Halton arose a complex of mills served by a mill race that extended for over half a mile. Five mills were constructed at Caton Town End, and the community outgrew the old township of Brookhouse. Mills for silk and flax have been recorded. In Dentdale, the main dale road beyond the village keeps close company with the River Dee, which turned the waterwheels at five corn mills when every tenant of a manor was obliged to take his corn to be ground at the manorial mill. The oldest was Nether Mill, standing near the bridge over the Dee near to Dent Town. No traces of the mill remain. J. Somevell, who made a study of water power in Westmorland in 1930, reported on a meeting he had with James Nelson Hayhurst, the jolly miller at Lupton, near Kirkby Lonsdale. The name of Hayhurst became as closely associated with northern milling as Tallon and Faraday were with the trade of blacksmith. Somevell discovered that in 1301 there was a Commission to Hugh de Louther and another to try a complaint of Matthew de Redman against 'persons who threw down his mill at Lupton, broke the dam and a boat, burnt his barn and assaulted David le Mareschal, his servant, etc., while he was on the King's Service'. James Hayhurst prepared oatmeal and, prior to the Second World War, sold it at places as far apart as Skipton and Barrow-in-Furness. Farmers who brought in oats they had grown might have them dried out and processed. At the mill were three pairs of stones – French burr, silver-grey Kellett and Derbyshire – and James also ground wheat, barley, corn, peas and beans. After scrubland round Lupton Mill was taken in and cultivated, sheep were kept and the wool processed at the mill before being taken by pack pony to Bradford. With the land under cultivation, the mill was converted to the processing of corn. One of Mr Hayhurst's predecessors, who lived in Mitchelgate at Kirkby Lonsdale, commuted to and from the mill on foot.

Davy Bank Mill, at Beckfoot in the upper Lune Valley, was one of dozens of little mills serving rural areas within living memory. With a good head of water in winter, the waterwheel's power was directed towards the grinding of oats and barley, some of it for domestic use and some as feeding stuffs for farm stock. Local milling suffered from the decline in ploughing and provision by large non-local firms of 'compound' feeding stuffs, which led in due course to bulk deliveries. A quarter of a century ago, Ernest Middleton lived in Pool House, just across the beck from the mill. He had been born in the house in 1909 and was the third generation of his family to work Davy Bank Mill. His grandfather John Middleton arrived here from the parish of Preston Patrick in 1888, and when he died in 1905 Edward, one of his three sons, took over. On his death, in 1926, the business descended to Ernest, who said that in the old days there was a mill such as Davy Bank within six or eight miles, 'whichever way you went'.

Before Ernest Middleton was 12 years of age he was sent out with horse and cart to deliver feed stuffs – maize meal, ground linseed, whole linseed, barley meal for the pigs, bran and crushed oats for the horses. Oats for human consumption was contained in ten stone bags. Maize, four tons at a time, was purchased from Liverpool and came straight from the docks. The Middletons ground it and made it into maize meal. Bran and 'thirds' came from flour millers at Bootle. A good deal of whole maize was sold for feeding to hens. The waterwheel at Davy Bank had a diameter of 13 feet and with a good flow of water was capable of generating from eight to ten horsepower. It rarely needed attention. Just after the First World War, a local joiner fitted some new spokes of pitch pine and the buckets were renovated. The main problem was that the stream had a small catchment area and was soon up and down, there being no dam. Two sets of stones were in use. One set, of French burrs, was used for grinding maize and barley, and a set of Derbyshire Peaks was ideal for grinding oats, the stone being appreciably softer than that of French origin. The stones were dressed, a summer occupation, as a prelude to the oatmeal season. A prized blacksmith was one who could temper a mill-bill, a type of pick used to attend to the grooves on a grindstone.

The mill could be a chilly place in winter, unless the worker was attending to the kiln, which was warmed by a large coke fire. The millers wore clogs, which were vital on the hot floor of the drying kiln. Clogs were also a boon in frosty weather. Threshing of corn began about October. The product was collected by horse-drawn carts and the initials of a farmer put on the bags intended for him, an example being JW for John Wooff. The number of bags intended for him was also indicated, and the letters 'rld' put on sacks where the corn had been rolled.

Before the First World War, oats were purchased at a street market in Penrith. In particular demand was a quality type known as 'potato oats' which had very little husk. The sacks of sample grain were placed on ladder-like structures to raise them above the ground and keep them dry. Any purchases by the Middletons were taken to Penrith station, off-loaded at Lowgill, and conveyed to Davy Bank Mill by horse and cart. During the war farmers grew their own oats and the miller's trade suffered. Davy Bank processed a farmer's oats – who promptly took them away once they had been dealt with.

Attached to the mill was a small farm of just two fields, in one of which a milk cow grazed. Occasionally, two cows were there. Two pigs were kept, the pork being for family consumption. Ernest's mother made butter and any surplus, in the form of round pounds, was collected along with spare eggs, by 'Butter Jack' (Jack Ward) of Sedbergh. He paid 8d. a pound. Ernie Middleton was born and lived at Davy Bank for almost eighty years until his death in 1989. He was fond of recalling that in the early 1920s the Middletons were the first people in the district to own a motor vehicle, a Ford used for transporting their goods. Ernie ran the family business with his mother and sister, and also kept the mill operating during the depressed 1930s; he also delivered coal, which he bagged up at Lowgill railway station.

After the Second World War, milling and other country industries declined and adaptations had to be made. Using his Ford vehicle, Ernie transported sheep and later cattle for local farmers. In 1951 he purchased a Morris wagon which should have had double wheels on the back. The need to cross the 6ft 6in wide Lune Bridge meant the vehicle was specially adapted, with single wheels and slimmer mudguards, and the distinctive wagon was soon a familiar sight along the roads of Howgill, Sedbergh, Firbank, Lambrigg and Grayrigg.

Phil Hudson, who carried out intensive research into quarrying and extractive industries in the Lune Valley, found that 'almost every farm, common, upland moorland or fell area has evidence of man's exploitation of material in the solid and drift geology'. Why? 'Most stone was not usually carried very far from its quarry source.' In the field boundary walls of the Lune Valley it is possible to see a wide date-range of local stone of various qualities. Contrasting with the abundant small field quarries was the grand-scale venture at Hutton Roof, a village that straddles a road beginning near the *Sportsman's Inn* and ending at Lupton. The large crag overshadowing the village was quarried in a period of boisterous activity that ended with the closure of the last two quarries in 1911. Land round Nanny Hall was formerly an unenclosed common, supporting several quarries and coal pits. The most celebrated quarries yielded grindstone with a special quality that gave a keen and fine edge to the best cutting tools without injuring the temper of the steel. Larger grindstones, up to three or four tons in weight, were in wide demand for smoothing steel needed for cutting tools and for polishing fenders, bright goods and steel fire irons.

Excavation costs were high, especially where water had to be pumped clear of the workings and transporting grindstones down narrow winding roads to railway stations could be frustrating. Thick beds of unprofitable 'shiver' (shale) were encountered. Grindstone and white freestone rock was worked in what was known as Old (or Township) Quarry; blue freestone rock, flags and grindstones were taken at Bowness's, Atkinson's and North's; grindstone alone was lifted from Moss Lot's Quarry. White freestone was excavated at the appropriately named White Quarry, and at Longfield Quarry (on Biggin's Hall estate) and Croftends Quarries. Red freestone was taken from Brownbank. Two properties yielded brittle coal.

Old Township, by far the oldest quarry, was worked in shares, or lots, but when this system proved unsatisfactory the quarry was let by tender to an individual firm, or quarry master. The stone was lifted by primitive methods until hand-powered cranes were installed, and for the last few years costly steam derricks were in use. Incidentally, when the Thirlmere-Manchester water supply flowed in a mile-long tunnel through the Crag in Victorian times, piped water became available in Hutton Roof. One old lady did not like the taste and said she preferred pump water.

Arten Gill, in the upper valley of the Dee, was noted for the so called Dent Marble, the trade name for several varieties of limestone quarried and polished in the Dent district. It was a dark limestone with fossils in a contrasting light shade. When, in the 1860s, the Midland Railway Company decided to extend a line northwards from Settle, what had – for transport reasons – been a largely local trade was expanded and large quantities of marble were soon being transported by train from the high-lying Dent station, two miles away. Swift expansion of the Stone House Works in Arten Gill resulted. The black marble was easily sawn unto blocks using water power. Marble fireplace surrounds were popular, both locally and in London, and Dent Marble formed the staircase of Owen's College, Manchester. The boom lasted until about 1899 when the removal of the tariff on Italian marble made quarrying in the dale unprofitable.

Samples of polished Dentdale marble appeared in a case at the London Law Courts. When the Midland tried to construct a viaduct at Denthead, an offer of £300 for a strip of land they required was made to the dalesman who owned it. The astute landowner was not tempted and the matter went to court and after much argument the railway company had to pay £1,600. This

126 *Jonty Wilson, blacksmith at Kirkby Lonsdale.*

figure pleased the dalesman, who had bought the entire farm for about £500
a few years previously.

William George Armstrong, founder of the great engineering works on
Tyneside, owed much to his early experience of the Arten Gill industry. In
1834, at the age of 24, he married Margaret Ramshaw and in 1835 took her
for a holiday to Yorkshire, angling in the River Dee. Entering Arten Gill,
he was impressed by the marble works and, in particular, by an enormous

waterwheel enclosed in a two-storey building that powered the machinery used for sawing and polishing. According to the historian Arthur Raistrick, Armstrong may have known of the works before his visit, for a Newcastle friend called John Blackmore, a civil engineer, was the son-in-law of the owner. Armstrong became interested in the use of water power and when his inquiries led him to believe that only about one twentieth of the available power of the beck was being used, his thoughts turned to hydraulic power. He studied the subject on his return to Newcastle and his interest was the start of what grew into the enormous Armstrong works.

Lunesdale coal was of a moderate quality. Thin seams of brittle, sulphurous stuff were abstracted via adits or shallow pits. The coal-working sites were widespread, with occasional groupings at named pit sites. Here the seams of coal were near to the surface, lodged between differing grit strata. John Phillips (1837) wrote that 'Most of the high ground between the Northern Yorkshire Dales, which is formed of Millstone Grit, yields Coal of such quality as to be serviceable in Lime Burning and, in the absence of better, for all the ordinary purposes of fuel.' The coal being slow-burning, a fire attended to in the morning would last until afternoon.

Mines existed on Barbon High Fell during the reign of Charles I, and these workings yielded coal between 1750 and 1860. The Kirkby Lonsdale parish register of 1761 noted the burial of John Frankland, a stranger, who died 'by falling into a coal pit near Barbon'. The *Lancaster Guardian* for 1831 recorded the death of Adam Braithwaite, a collier at Barbon who was buried when the roof of the working collapsed. Coal was still worked not far from Easegill up to the mid-1940s. Sedbergh-Dowbiggin workings were opened up about 1760 and closed in 1855. Casterton, with its mixture of bell-pits, shafts and adits, was worked from 1650 to 1860. Mining ceased at the Garsdale and Dent pits with the opening of the Settle-Carlisle railway, when deep-mined coal from South Yorkshire became available. A dalesman who died in 1929 aged 83 recalled that he began work in Wold Pit, Garsdale at the age of nine, and had to provide his own candles and knee-pads. The tubs were pulled out of the workings by men moving on hands and knees. During winter, the only daylight the man saw was on Sundays.

Before good roads gave villagers ready access to the nearest town each village had a range of crafts, and when the horse was master of the dusty road the blacksmith throve. In 1907 Jonty Wilson, aged 14, began work at a blacksmith's shop in Kirkby Lonsdale. His first job was to collect horses and lead them to the smithy for re-shoeing. The arrangement meant the smithy did not become congested. Visiting the stables as early as 5.45 a.m. he would check the horses and put a chalk mark on any needing attention. At the smithy, three fires were operating.

Being a major centre in upper Lunesdale, Kirkby Lonsdale had a range of tradesmen, most of whom owned a horse and vehicle: bakers and butchers had vans; the doctor kept a small phaeton; and the veterinary surgeon preferred a small four-wheeler. The blacksmith corrected faults in a horse's gait and coped with all manner of foot ailments, the most common of which were corns, bruised soles, punctures, ring-bone and side-bone. More severe diseases were navicular, which affected the bones of the foot and was caused by concussion, and laminitis, a fever in the foot, usually a consequence of an inappropriate diet.

Joe Tallon, blacksmith at Lupton for over sixty years, was 11 years old when he started work. He earned 10s. a week, which was considered good for a youngster. It was nearly all horse work but Joe frequently stayed at the smithy until nine o'clock at night, sharpening plough irons. There were no wheels on ploughs at that time, and the irons had to be regularly trimmed. Anyone working 'sharp' land needed to have them trimmed every other day. Joe could turn his hand to almost anything. He made new fenders for Westmorland firesides, each weighing as much as could be lifted. He removed 'wolf-teeth' from the mouths of horses with a hammer and chisel. Only one hit was possible as the horse would not tolerate a second attempt!

Chapter 9

Education, Sport and Pastimes

Queen Elizabeth School at Kirkby Lonsdale is a much-respected 11-18 co-educational and non-denominational comprehensive school with over 1,400 pupils. Two-thirds of its population are drawn from outside the original Cumbria catchment area – from Sedbergh, Ingleton, Lancaster, Arnside and Kendal. The school site, on the edge of Kirkby Lonsdale, is extensive, and landscaping projects have given it form, shape and coherence. They have added avenues, courtyards, gardens and an amphitheatre. This school is the largest employer in the town.

A Grammar School founded at Kirkby Lonsdale in 1591 was sited in Mill Brow. Along with Kendal School, it was endowed with scholarships to Queen's College, Oxford. Records left by William Wolfenden, who emigrated to Canada and recollected his life at Kirkby Lonsdale in the 1850s, give an illuminating account of school life in Victorian days. The Rev. Thomas Croft was Master when Mr Wolfenden started as a foundation boy in 1854. A stern disciplinarian, he was expert with the cane, which rarely left his hand during the school day. Mr Wolfenden was initiated into the Latin grammar but never saw an English grammar in the school and remained ignorant of the subject to his dying day.

Sedbergh School, founded by Roger Lupton in 1525, casts an aura over the town in which it is a major property owner. Its dozen rugby fields and the broad sweep of a cricket field near St Andrew's Church ensure the town does not look congested. Two of seven large houses associated with the school lie in Sedbergh itself. A former school uniform was known as 'the Blues' and made up of blue shirts and blue blazer, with long blue stockings. Lupton's original chantry school was 'for the maintaining and increase of learning in Christ's Church' and for the health of Lupton's soul. An agreement was made that the Chaplain and Scholars should have free seats in the chancel of

127 *Old School (now the Library), Sedbergh School.*

the parish church. Lupton, a native of Cautley, obtained a Bachelor of Laws degree at King's College, Cambridge, and subsequently became a Canon of Windsor (1500) and Provost of Eton College (1504).

The foundation deed bound the School to St John's College, Cambridge, which appointed its Headmasters. This connection was the chantry's salvation when other chantries were being dissolved and their assets seized in the reign of Henry VIII. The Master pleaded that the School was needed in the north country, 'amongst the rude people in knowledge'. Sedbergh became a Grammar School in 1551. In the 1660s Edward Fell did much to revive its fortunes, sending 81 boys to Cambridge and leaving five pounds in his will, the interest from which was to be used for the purchase of dictionaries. In the same decade, under the headship of Samuel Saunders, the New School House (now the Library) was built. During the headship of Wynne Bateman (1746-82), the School achieved fame at Cambridge, its boys excelling in Classics and Mathematics.

John Dawson (1734-1820), a native of Garsdale, was to play a significant part in the history of Sedbergh School. He became distinguished both as a mathematician and surgeon and as mentor of Adam Sedgwick, the geologist. After studying medicine at Edinburgh he returned to Garsdale and made a living as a tutor of Mathemetics at Sedbergh. As a private tutor at Cambridge between 1781 and 1807, he coached 12 Senior Wranglers. Hartley Coleridge, son of the celebrated poet, was a tutor at Sedbergh for a brief period and assumed the headship temporarily on the death of Henry Wilkinson. Hartley was fond of the Sedbergh area, especially its hills and rivers, and, quoting Homer, said they were 'the colour of old port'. Small in stature, he often sat among the boys on one of the school benches – in the recollection of one of his students. His odd antics, such as turning up for classes late and leaving early, and his fondness for drink, led to the school governors dispensing with his services.

During the time when John Harrison Evans was Head, from 1838 until 1861, 480 boys entered the school and a high standard of scholarship was achieved. The town of Sedbergh benefited from his efforts and generosity, specifically with the erection of the Market Hall and Reading Room. The school has had its 'downs' as well as 'ups', and under Henry George Day, a scholar who failed to inspire, the number of scholars subsequently shrank to fifteen. He resigned with a large pension. Local patriotism and the loyalty of Old Boys saved the school from losing its identity and a revival began under the headship of Frederick Heppenstall (1875-9). Towards the end of

128 *Chapel interior, Sedbergh School.*

129 *Powell Hall, Sedbergh School.*

this period, the Governors instructed the architects Austin and Paley of Lancaster to produce a plan for a range of new buildings, the cost to be met by generous benefactors. The most notable, Sir Francis Sharp Powell, Chairman of the Governors, had a major building named after him. The new Chapel was constructed in 1897.

Among many innovations at Sedbergh was the introduction of rugby football and school songs. Logie Bruce Lockhart, presenting some Sedbergh School songs in *The Dalesman*, observed that in a school which, given its size, has probably produced more rugby internationals than any other, it is not surprising the rugby song is the best known:

> The sunshine is melting the snow on the Calf,
> And the Rawthey is loud in the dale,
> And there seems every chance of our getting a 'half',
> If the weather glass tells a true tale.
> What shall we do with it? Suck lollipops?
> Swelter and sicken till tea?
> Loaf in the town and lounge in the shops?
> Waste money and muscle? Not we!

130 *Headmaster's House, Sedbergh School.*

The Wilson Run cross-country race, an annual tradition that began in 1881, is held at the end of the Lent term. The steeplechase of 10 miles takes its name from Bernard Wilson, a master who made scholars aware of the countryside lying beyond the town by encouraging them to explore it. In 1993 Charles Sykes became the record holder when he completed the course in 1 hour 8 minutes and 4 seconds. The Memorial Cloisters, completed in 1924, were designed by J. Hubert Worthington, an Old Sedberghian. They were renovated in 2005. Sedbergh School became co-educational in 2001 when Lupton House was reopened as a girls' house.

Casterton School, for girls, has a sylvan setting and handsome range of buildings on a 50 acre site a short distance from Kirkby Lonsdale. Over 300 pupils benefit from the excellent boarding and educational facilities. The Rev. William Carus Wilson, a rather dour but caring Evangelical clergyman, established Casterton as an educational centre. The first school existed for the benefit of servants and teachers, and there followed at Cowan Bridge a Clergy Daughters' School, where girls were educated at low cost. The Carus family held land in the reign of Edward II and subsequently possessed estates in Melling, Arkholme, Wrayton and Whittington. William Carus Wilson, father of the founder of the school, was educated at Queen Elizabeth's School,

Kirkby Lonsdale, and later at Trinity College, Cambridge, graduating in 1786. Jane M. Ewbank, who researched the family and in particular the life of William Carus Wilson, notes that at Cambridge he came under the influence of the evangelical Charles Simeon, whose religious outlook was derived from 16th-century Calvinism, which inspired 'a fear of hell, a shuddering horror of sin and a faith that would remove mountains'.

The Brontë connection was a result of the death of Patrick's wife, after which he shed some family responsibilities by sending daughters Marie, Elizabeth, Charlotte and Emily to the Cowan Bridge school in 1824-5. The nucleus of the school was a house, adapted for the use of the teachers, on to which were built at right angles a long annexe for the schoolroom and the pupils' dormitories. The grim winter of 1824-5 was the only one during which the children had to walk about two and a half miles every Sunday to Tunstall church to attend the morning and afternoon services, the reason being the temporary closure of Leck church. Between the Tunstall services, a cold lunch was served in a small room over the porch which was entered then via a balcony. Nowadays the more athletic clamber up a ladder fixed to the wall to enter a small room with a single small window.

On her admittance to the school, it was said of Charlotte that she writes indifferently, 'ciphers a little and works neatly. Knows nothing of grammar, geography, history of accomplishments.' In this she was not alone, and it is to the credit of the staff that she became an accomplished writer and had the confidence to apply for the position of governess. Charlotte's subsequent

131 *Clergy Daughters' School, now a row of cottages, Cowan Bridge.*

account in one of her novels of the hard, unsympathetic life at the Cowan Bridge school was doubtless exaggerated, but schools of that period were inclined to impose harsh discipline on those attending. The school became 'Lowood' in *Jane Eyre*. Tunstall church became Brocklebridge church. Charlotte gives a chilling account of school life and wrote of Mr Brocklehurst, the headmaster of her fictional school, 'He is not a god, nor is he even a great and admired man; he is little liked here; he never took steps to make himself liked.' Miss M. Williams, a former headmistress, researched the school's history in the 1930s and comments, 'It can hardly be doubted, I think, that the site was not very wisely chosen, and that the buildings when ready were cold, bare and dull, and lacking much of what is considered absolutely necessary in the

132 *Ladder leading to room above porch at Tunstall church, where Clergy Daughters dined.*

present, but that Mr Carus Wilson should be blamed and abused because he was not ahead of his time in the internal economy of a School seems to me very hard on the memory of a good man, who devoted himself, his influence and his money to the schools at Tunstall and at Cowan Bridge.' In any case, immediately after its foundation the property of the School was transferred to 12 Trustees.

Charlotte is said to have found pleasure in sitting by the river listening to the chuckle of water that had come straight from the fells. There is a stony bed, which explains the local saying: 'as rough as Leck Beck Bottom'. In Charlotte's day, the coach that ran between Leeds and Kendal creaked and groaned as it was drawn over the rutted stretch of local road. The Brontës would see wool buyers from their native West Riding heading for the farms of Cumberland and Westmorland. The Trustees of the School would doubtless worry about the close connection between traffic and the safety of their charges.

During the spring of 1825 a low fever broke out at the school. Maria Brontë was sent home on February 14, only to die at Haworth on 6 May. Elizabeth was sent home, seriously ill, on 31 May and Charlotte and Emily were transferred to the seaside home of the Wilsons at Silverdale. It was customary for some girls to spend the summer break from lessons at this holiday home, Carus Wilson charging a small fee. The Brontë girls were there for a single night as Patrick arrived to collect them next day and thus ended their stay at the school.

The accommodation at the Clergy Daughters' School proving to be inadequate and inconvenient, it was re-established in a new building at Casterton in 1832, originally with 90 pupils drawn from all over the world as the Church Missionary Society was paying for the education of the daughters of missionaries. Holy Trinity Church at Casterton was built on the instructions of Carus Wilson and was shared, from the beginning, by the school and the community. The windows of the chancel, installed in the 1890s, were the work of Henry Holiday of Hampstead, a stained glass artist of considerable repute. Carus Wilson was buried on land at the back of the church and once a year, on Founder's Day, wreaths are laid on behalf of the school. In 1921 the School was amalgamated with another one situated not far away, which existed for 'the training of Servants and Teachers'. It retains a firm Anglican attachment and words written by Miss Williams in 1935 are still apt. Referring to the little Clergy Daughters' School started in a remote corner of Lancashire and subsequently moving to Westmorland, she said, 'It has developed as the present-day, well-equipped, up-to-date Casterton School.'

Social life was largely ordered by ancient custom. On Easter Monday people converged on Sellet Banks, a prominent hill midway between Kirkby Lonsdale and Whittington, to roll hard-boiled eggs on the slopes in competition with the Whittington folk. The eggs were subsequently broken

133 *Old engraving of west front, Casterton School.*

and the contents eaten. Each child received an orange. The menfolk of Lupton and Hutton Roof joined those from Endmoor and Gatebeck to play 'knurr and spell' on Lupton's Pleasure Ground, the 'poor' field of the parish which was let every year to the highest bidder. The men made their own sticks and 'pum' heads. A ball fashioned from wood was set on a spring and when the player was ready he tapped the spring with the pum head. The ball went up and had to be hit on the way down, or the player was considered 'out'. The balls being used by the best exponents travelled scores of yards.

Sedbergh had its own pack of foxhounds, the huntsman being Matt Sedgwick. On one occasion the fox led the pack from Four Lane Ends in Howgill, over Black Force and across Grains Ghyll, where it went to earth and had to be dug out. Joe Bowman, huntsman with the Ullswater pack of foxhounds, would base them on Sedbergh for a week. The hounds were 'kysty', or fastidious, and quickly detected if the meal being served to them had been mixed with blue, or skimmed, milk. If blue milk alone was available, someone was sent to the next farm for milk. On the day when the fox was killed on the crag at Cautley, the hunt ended up at *The Cross Keys*, where punch was brewed and stirred with the fox's brush. When Mrs Sedgwick, the landlady, became aware of what was happening, the hunting party was hustled off to the kitchen to be fed on milk and apple pasty.

134 *Old print of Casterton.*

In autumn, thoughts of the gentry turned to the mass destruction of reared pheasants. On the death of the Earl of Bective in 1893, Lady Henry Cavendish-Bentink had become tenant for life at Underley Hall and its vast estate. Financial support was provided by gilt-edged securities that produced an income equivalent to that derived from the land. Aristocratic visitors to Underley during the pheasant-shooting season included Edward VII. Unofficial visitors were poachers, many of whom were driven to act through hunger. A poacher in pheasant country would feed pheasants for a few days with corn, then attach paper bags to the ground with wire, having daubed the inside of each bag with syrup overspread with oats. When a pheasant attempted to reach the oats the bag would stick to its head and it was easily caught. A soundless method of poaching was to use a catapult. Hares, which kept slavishly to certain runs, were netted using a 'gate' or purse net. A long net was dragged across fields to envelop roosting partridges.

The Duke of Portland considered the pheasant shooting in the country round Lupton the best in all England. Lord Henry Bentinck's idea was to make the shooting as difficult as possible. He did not want to stand on top of the birds and slaughter them so they were encouraged to fly high. Lord Henry had sciatica and was conveyed to the copses in a four-wheeled carriage. He was so pleased one morning when 1,000 pheasants were shot before lunch that tears ran down his face. One guest shot 96 pheasants in one stand. The names of the guns in 1902 were the Duke of Portland, Lord Elcho, Lord Charles Bentinck, Captain Lindsay, Mr Somers Somerset, Colonel Rhodes, the Hon. G Gore, and Lord Henry. Several gamekeepers reared and protected the pheasants, and between 80 and 90 beaters were employed, their white jackets being dried in the evening ready for the next day.

135 *The Brontë School at Cowan Bridge.*

136a *Mrs Carus Wilson, Casterton School.*

The head forester, a Scotsman, kept the beaters under strict control, marching them in line through the woods. A beater earned 3s. 6d. a day, and his lunch. The shooters drove up in carriage and four while a man, sometimes a farmer's son, carried the cartridge bags and a valet did the loading. Mr Woodhouse from Kirkby Lonsdale took away most of the pheasants for sale. It was said that 'Up went £1 (the pheasant). Bang went a penny (the cartridge). And down went half a crown (the dead bird).'

Kit Wilson of Rigmaden welcomed his friend Colonel Marton of Capernwray for the main pheasant shoot, the Colonel arriving by coach and four. Greeting the Colonel, Kit said he was sorry that the gardener was ill, which was news to the Colonel who had spoken to him that morning. But Kit, accustomed to seeing his visitor's large retinue and familiar with the grand style of Lunesdale squires, said, 'I thought your gardener couldn't be well as you haven't brought him.'

When it was suspected that poachers were operating, police and gamekeepers patrolled the woods. A poacher might avoid being caught with prey by hiding dead pheasants in pre-arranged spots, the wives of the poachers walking that way next day with prams. On the return journey the children had feather mattresses. A popular night for poaching pheasants was 5 November, when fireworks were exploding and no one was likely to notice an extra bang or two from the woods where pheasants roosted. On still, misty nights, poachers would crawl quietly to the base of the trees where pheasants roosted and burn cob sulphur, which stupefied the birds. A sack was sometimes employed to waft the fumes upwards. Some men threaded horse hair through small peas and left them at the feeding grounds.

The Lune was a prime salmon river. *Salmonidae of Westmorland* by George Foster Braithwaite, an early book on angling, was published at Kendal in 1884. Braithwaite states

136b *Rev. William Carus Wilson, Casterton School.*

137 *Cover of* Hints to Lunesdale Anglers.

that the bed of the Lune is rocky and gravelly, 'and with an admirable variety of torrent, stream and pool'. Giving a general idea of the river, he writes,

> Now we come to a stretch of deep water flowing quietly amidst banks shaded with trees, then to a sharp turn round which water swirls; a series of gravel beds follow, over which the stream trickles and murmers, and in the deeper portions of which are favourite haunts of smoults and trout. A rocky bed is now approached, over which the water roars and foams, or confined between the walls of a deep fissure, worn by ages to an unseen depth, glides along with majestic dignity.

138 *Lancashire River Board Hatchery, Upper Lune, 1964.*

Tom Bradley, in *Yorkshire Angler's Guide*, published in 1894, described the Lune as running down a beautiful valley which is enclosed by high mountains, the stream falling over a rocky limestone bed in a succession of streams and pools, and the trout fishing on the Lune as 'good' and the salmon fishing 'fairly decent'. The highest salmon net on the river was a little above Rawthey Mouth. As salmon could get up the whole length of the river, even as far as Ravenstonedale, the rod fishing was classifiable as 'good'.

The salmon season was short. The fish 'do not come up this part of the river until September, and the river suffers materially from snatching and spearing in the close time'. This, for salmon, was 15 November until 1 March. For trout, the dates were 2 October until 1 March. A rod licence for salmon cost 20s., and for trout 2s. 6d. Good salmon were caught in September and October. The trout averaged about three to the pound. Shorter days and low river temperatures galvanised salmon into greater activity by mid-November. Subtle hormone changes ripened the females, who then parted with their pink eggs at 'redds' made in the gravel beds of the headwaters. The flanks of an excited cock fish were mottled with yellow-orange and red, and from the lower jaw extended a hook, or 'kype'. They covered the eggs with fertilising milt. It has been this way on the Lune for some 10,000 years – the salmon establishing their spawning behaviour with the end of the Ice Age and the melting of the great valley glaciers. Each year a proportion of

139 *Cock salmon from the Lune.*

the Atlantic salmon stock that had gained weight and maturity in the deeps off Greenland fought its way to the headwaters of its native river and its tributary becks to ensure the contination of the race. The silver-blue bodies of the hen fish were packed with eggs: some 750 to every pound of body weight. In 1980 the water bailiff saw an immense 'redd' some 21 feet long and over four feet wide.

A shiver of excitement ran up the spine of a Lunedale poacher when he became aware the salmon were running. Using gaff or bull's-eye lantern, the poacher removed fish from the spawning grounds at the gravel beds. He had a lamp attached to his waist, a salmon remaining still when a beam of light falls upon it. Canon Rawnsley, Vicar of Crosthwaite and one of the founders of the National Trust, wrote:

> He who goes fishing in the Lune
> Without the aid of sun or moon,
> Needs not a rod, but wants a stick
> About his back, the lunatic!

Herbert Dean, who moved to Kirkby Lonsdale in 1888, took out a fishing licence in 1895 which was issued for the Lune, Wyre, Keer and Cocker Fishery District. Most local anglers dated their interest in fishy matters to the Rev. J.N. Williams, master at the Grammar School, who was keen on

140 *Fertilising salmon eggs at a Lunesdale hatchery.*

fishing for salmon. Ten pounds is the average weight of salmon, much bigger fish setting the tongues of the town wagging. Dean said that whenever the Rev. Williams caught a salmon the schoolboys were given a day off studies. His angling enthusiasm reached a high point on the day when, while fishing at the island during the dinner hour, he caught two of the lordly fish.

A Kirkby Lonsdale boy with an interest in angling might purchase a rod – of ash, with a lance-wood top – made by Herbert Wearing, the local joiner, for a price of ten shillings. When there was a freshet, Herbert Dean and two or three friends would visit the riverside in the morning to be sure of catching fish: 'At first we fished with worm. As the river cleared, we would fish minnow. Then, with the waters clearing still further, we'd fish fly. The river held its colour longer than it does today. Before roads were tarred, they got muddy. Now, with tarred roads and better drains, the river was apt to clear in a day.' Richard Garlick was known to haul out of the Lune at flood-time from sixty to seventy trout. Tom Preston, a local stonemason, carried his book of feathers and silks to the riverside so that he might dress a fly like the ones currently on the water. His son dressed the flies of local boy anglers. The charge was 1s. ½d. a time. 'We always practised on the island and reckoned that more flies were lost on the shingle than would stock a fishing tackler's shop.'

When there was a 'big watter' the Rawthey dashed to join up with the Lune at a gravelly area called The Meetings, half a mile below Broadraine. When the Lancashire River Board, keen to increase the number of salmon, had a salmon trap here in the 1960s, salmon were held briefly in a riverside coop before being transported to a hatchery at Middleton. Here, a hen fish was stripped of its eggs. It was held just short of the tail, and when it calmed down a rope was slipped around its head and settled behind the pectoral fins. The act of coaxing ova from a salmon involved the gentle application of pressure to the underside. A torrent of salmon eggs would pour into a

141 *The heron, a familiar waterside bird (by David Binns).*

plastic yellow bowl. In less than a minute the fish was a 'kelt' (spent fish) and allowed a period of recuperation before being returned to the river. A captive cock salmon provided the necessary dash of milt, which was mixed with river water before being applied to the eggs. These, fertilised, began to fill out and were then retained in containers made of mesh in a flow of water for the incubation period. This way they avoided the natural perils of river life.

Salmon eggs, when treated in a well-guarded manner, formed a potent bait for trout. It was not unusual in the later part of the 19th century for a basket of twenty brown trout to be collected using this lure. Herbert Dean walked home with a brown trout weighing two pounds and a sea trout that made the scales dip at three and a half pounds. An angler's wife who ordered sausages for Saturday lunch dashed to the butcher after the Lune came into flood and asking him to cancel the order, explaining 'George's gone fishing.'

Some of the poachers on the upper Lune used a 'leister', a three-pronged fork with a barb on each prong. Local people called the barb a 'wither'. Attached to a pole some six feet long, the' leister' came into play after light was directed on a salmon, thereby mesmerising it, the 'leister' then being plunged into the fish. A gaff, which was rather like a meat hook, might be attached to a stick. After a salmon had been hooked, it would be hauled in by a cord attached to the gaff itself. Another device consisted of barbs on a lead weight to keep it on the bed of a river. A cord was used to draw it through the water towards the luckless salmon or sea trout. The lamps used were of various types. The most unusual was a biscuit tin with sockets for half a dozen candles. One end of the tin was removed and a glass fitted. Worn around the neck by means of a piece of wire, the device might be used to direct light into the river while leaving the poacher's hands free for other tasks. If a shippon lamp were used, most of the glass was blackened, just a small area left clear. Light shining through this area was adequate for the job in hand.

Jonty Wilson was told of a 40 lb salmon poached from the Lune by men using gaffs and bull's eye lanterns. The poacher tied the lamp to a belt round his waist and moved slowly until the beam revealed a fish maintaining a fixed position. It was a simple matter, then, to 'click' it with the gaff. Fish were poached not so much for their cash value, few being sold, but because the poachers enjoyed testing their wits against river, salmon and the water bailiff. It was said that lads who poached salmon one snowy evening were so successful the sack into which the captive salmon were placed was almost too heavy to be carried. Sometimes a dead salmon was found on the bank. The fish had been taken by an otter which simply ate the heart, leaving the rest of the fish as food for any body or thing who chanced upon it.

Those bobbing for eels used a mess of worsted and worms plus a lead weight as the bob. Eel pie was a tasty dish. In the 1850s, according to notes kept by William Wolfenden, Kirkby Lonsdale lads regularly visited Terry Bank Tarn, a small, dark, brackish tarn on the moors near Old Town which was said to be the haunt of enormous eels, though none was caught. Wolfenden and friends, while out in a boat, reported seeing an eel some five feet long 'that appeared to have fins on either side of its head; they resembled big ears'. Few people believed them. Wolfenden heard from an employee at the corn mill operated by a stream from the tarn of a time when it overflowed its banks. Lying in a dry ditch was an eel said to have a length of eight or ten feet and a body as thick as the finder's leg. The Rev. J.J. Fisher, Vicar of Kirkby Lonsdale, sought monster eels with rod, then with night lines made of gut, and eventually with string and wire, but his efforts were in vain.

Crayfish were taken from the Spital beck by means of a quarter-inch riddle. Three holes were bored through the wooden frame at equal distance and strings connected to the handle to manipulate it in the water, then pieces of dead rabbit were placed in the riddle to attract the crayfish. Two colonies of native white crayfish in Lunesdale were saved from extinction in recent times through a costly project by a local group after it located the last remaining colonies in a small beck near Tebay and in a tributary that flows through Hornby. The Lune Habitat Group, in conjunction with the Environment Agency, has also targeted areas for the benefit of spawning fish, otters, water voles and pearl mussels.

Kirkby Lonsdale Angling Association was founded in 1928. The first president was, of course, Lord Henry Bentinck, of Underley Hall, and his wife was the patron. The Bentincks agreed to lease the Underley waters at an easy rent and so the Association secured the fishing along six miles and 365 yards, mostly on both banks. An Angling Club was formed at Tebay shortly after the Second World War and its members had rights on about ten miles of the river. Tom Davison, a railway signalman when I met him in the early 1950s, told me that in the early spring – from the middle of March onwards – an angler might expect to have good sport among the trout. The angling improved as the season progressed. Excellent sport followed a stonefly hatch, usually of ten days duration, in May. This was a time when freshets brought salmon to the upper reaches. It was held that on the upper Lune a salmon would not respond to a fly, but Tom's experiences belied this idea. He hooked a salmon weighing 21½ lb while fly-fishing. His chosen flies for salmon were Green Highlander, Silver Doctor and Jock Scott. Tom wrote a book entitled *Angler and Otter* wherein he related that he hooked a trout weighing 21lb 5oz; he had been using stonefly at Dillicar.

Letters written by Thomas Bowness Wright, of Gaisgill near Tebay, between 1917 until 1933 and mainly about natural history, were published in 1936 under the title *The Watcher by the Bridge*. In 1920 Wright hooked and landed a sea trout weighing ten ounces. He regularly strolled down to the bridge of the title of the book and more than once watched otters searching for food. He was fond of fishing a black fly 'with wings made from the shining feather of a rook, which I expect they take for a beetle. I have made them from a magpie feather but I don't think they like them any better than rook.'

Falconry was another popular sport among the gentry, and the knightly family of Middleton held their lands in the Lune Valley by rendering a yearly tribute of a 'cast' of falcons to the over-lord of Kendal Castle. Eyases, or nestlings, were procured from Kingsdale and Dentdale. The young of dainty

142 *Vale of Lune Harriers, at a Meet in 1963 (by Edward Jeffrey).*

merlins, the smallest of the falcons and a ground-nesting species, came from Leck Fell. Owls, both Barn and Long-eared, were flown over the meadows at dusk for voles and rats. They were much easier to train and handle than the falcons. A character known as Deadwood Dick kept falcons, hawks and owls in the Kirkby Lonsdale area. As a young lad in the early 1900s, Jonty Wilson helped him with the feeding and flying of birds. The falconer had studied the subject during 21 years' service with the Army, mostly in northern India and the Far East. The birds were housed in a loft over a wash-house in Biggins and were flown at every type of quarry. Jonty recalled flying a falcon on the fells in the early morning, when he would imitate the call of a cock grouse and loose the falcon jesses as another grouse came to investigate.

In the period between the wars, Mr Punchard, agent for the prestigious Underley Estate, resided in an impressive Victorian house known as The Gables. His wife, Constance, a native of Milnthorpe, was a novelist who wrote under her maiden name of Holme and based her stories in Westmorland. She penned short stories and eight novels which had the distinction of being included in the *Worlds Classic* series published by Oxford University Press.

143   *Curlew, familiar breeding bird on the uplands.*

Chapter 10

Modern Times

Prior to the boundary changes of 1974, a stranger visiting the upper Lune Valley would have been at a loss to know in which county he or she was standing. The Rev. John C. Bacon, who had the spiritual oversight of three parishes – Howgill in Yorkshire, and Firbank and Killington in Westmorland – ministered in the Deanery of Sedbergh and the Diocese of Bradford, although the city of Bradford, with its cathedral, lay 62 miles away. Between his Vicarage at Firbank and Holy Trinity Church at Howgill lay five miles of tortuous narrow road.

A profound change within the Yorkshire Dales National Park came in the year 2000 with the Countryside and Rights of Way Act. The area of open access land rose from four to sixty per cent of the Park. In January 2008 a radical proposal to enlarge the National Park was put out to public consultation. Natural England, the government agency charged with exploring the possibility of extending this and the Lake District National Park, set a timetable for consultation. If the enlargement comes into effect, the Yorkshire Dales National Park will be extended to absorb Mallerstang and Wild Boar Fell, the northern Howgills, parts of the Lune Valley (including Kirkby Lonsdale), and Firbank, Middleton, Barbon and Leck Fells. Orton Fells would become part of the Dales Park or be designated an Area of Outstanding Natural Beauty outside the Park. The idea of this extension was put forward in 2005 by the Countryside Agency, which has since been absorbed by Natural England.

When local government boundaries were revised, Kirkby Lonsdale and adjacent parts of Lunesdale which were previously in Westmorland were included in the new county of Cumbria. Sedbergh, formerly in the West Riding of Yorkshire, was also transferred to Cumbria, while perversely retaining a link with Yorkshire Dales National Park. David Leather, author of a book of walks, aptly notes that the area takes its character from both counties, while retaining a distinctive quality. Those who visit the area today will see signs of change and decay but the overall impression is of rural people ungrudgingly adapting to modern ideas and tending the landscape in a complementary way. Through the Lune Gorge, where once passed Roman soldiers, pedlars, packmen and drovers moving cattle from Scotland, considerably more traffic travels noisily along the M6. The 'whoosh' of express trains attaining high speed on an electrified line is muffled by the steady roar of adjacent road traffic. The level of sound from the motorway varies with the weather conditions, but on some days it is loud enough to drown the whistled commands of a hill farmer to his dog as they gather sheep on the nearby fell.

In the late 1960s and early 1970s the new road through the Lune Gorge transformed local life and enabled tourist services, such as catering, to flourish. The old road, over Shap, ran against the 'grain' of the landscape. The construction of the M6 demanded a workforce of about 1,000 and 33 months of intensive work, day and night, in 12 hour shifts. The contractors first built a six-mile access road and along it came special equipment – over 250 items of large plant, including 35 ton Euclid trucks. Twenty bridges were needed and three of them were valued at over £500,000 each. One of the nineteen box culverts is three-quarters of a mile long. The existing A685 was re-routed along a ledge cut specially from the fellside. Rail traffic was protected by special blasting techniques and the erection of three miles of anti-submarine type netting and nylon mesh. Eight underbridges were needed to carry the motorway two and a half miles at one point, and three more carried the diverted A685. The Borrowbeck viaduct has a maximum height of 73 feet.

Another of the challenges the M6 presented to engineers was the construction of an interchange on the Tebay flood plain below the village. Over a million cubic yards of fill were tipped in order to lift the road surface above the highest known flood level of a river that might rise 12 feet after torrential rainfall on the fells. Blasting and other operations during the construction period were incessant. A local farmer commented, 'For two or three years, we didn't hear a lamb bleat or birds sing.' The coming of the motorway led to the demolition of a cottage from which, until 1932, a railway signalman regularly sauntered to the old 'block cabin' at Dillicar, where he watched the passage of over 70 trains, all 'steamers', in an eight-hour shift. Today, with its sweeping curves and backdrop of the Howgill Fells, the M6 is among the most scenically attractive stretches of motorway in the land.

Bibliography

Banks, John, *The Silent Stream: A History of Grisdale* (1991)

Bonser, K.J., *The Drovers* (1970)

Boulton, David and Anthea, *In Fox's Footsteps* (1998)

Bowker, Sheila, *The Three Peaks and the Howgill Fells* (2006)

Bryer, T. Percy, *A History of Methodism in Kendal, Kirkby Lonsdale and Sedbergh* (1987)

Collingwood, W.G., *The Lake Counties* (1902)

Collins, Herbert C., *Lancashire Plain and Seaboard* (1953)

Duerden, Norman, *Portrait of the Dales* (1978)

Ffinch, Michael, *Portrait of the Howgills and the Upper Eden Valley* (1982)

Garlick, Tom, *Romans in the Lake Counties* (1970); *Roman Lancashire* (1977)

Gresson, Mary, *A Stroll Through Kirkby Lonsdale* (1996)

Joy, David, *The Lake Counties: Regional Railways* (1983)

Hall, Michael J., *Old Kirkby Lonsdale and the Rainbow Parish* (2004)

Hartley, Marie and Ingilby, Joan, *The Old Handknitters of the Dales* (1951, new edition 2001)

Hindle, Brian Paul, *Roads and Trackways of the Lake District* (1984)

Leather, A. David, *The Walker's Guide to the Howgills and Dentdale* (1993)

Mitchell, W.R., *A Cumbrian Blacksmith: Jonty Wilson* (1978); *High Dale Country* (1991)

Mitchell, W.R. and Swallow, Bob, *The Walker's Guide to South-East Lakeland* (1997)

Moorhouse, Sydney, *Holiday Lancashire* (1955)

Nicholson, Norman, *Cumberland and Westmorland (1949)*; *Portrait of the Lakes* (1963); *Greater Lakeland* (1969)

Palmer, J.H., *Historic Farmhouses in and around Westmorland* (1952)

Palmer, William T., *The Verge of Lakeland* (1938)

Pearson, Alexander, *The Doings of a Country Solicitor* (1947)

Rollinson, William, *A History of Man in the Lake District* (1967)

Rowling, Marjorie, *The Folklore of the Lake District* (1976)

Sale, Geoffrey, *The History of Casterton School* (1983)

Savage, E.U. (ed.), *The Watcher by the Bridge: letters of Thomas Bowness Wright* (1936)

Shotter, David, and White, Andrew, *The Romans in Lunesdale* (1995)

Speakman, Colin, *Adam Sedgwick: Geologist and Dalesman* (1982)

Thompson, Rev. W, *Three Picturesque Yorkshire Dales* (1910)

Trott, Stan and Freda, *Return to the Lune Valley* (1972)

Wainwright, Alfred, *Walks on the Howgill Fells* (1972)

Waterhouse, John, *The Stone Circles of Cumbria* (1985)

Wellburn, Alan R., *Leck, Cowan Bridge and the Brontës* (1997)

Westall, Oliver M. (general editor), *From Lancaster to the Lakes* (Lancaster University, 1992)

Williams, M., *Notes on the Clergy Daughters' School, Casterton* (1935)

Winstanley, Michael (ed.), *Rural Industries of the Lune Valley* (2000)

Woodger, Phyllis L. and Hunter, Jessie E., *The High Chapel, Ravenstonedale* (2nd edition, 1987)

Index

Bank

Hill Castle

Stone Hall

Hollin Hill

Loc Low Bank

Low Thorns

Strait Bridge

Gunrow

Green Mos

SEDBERGH

Brig Hall

Turnpike

Lane End Side

Hall Bank

Garsdale

Rigg Dale Foot

Hill Top

White Beck Hole

Nether

Birks

Quakers Meeting

Mill

Hill Hall

Moorthw

iddle Holme

High Holme

Mashers

Mayer Hill

Rash House

Cote

DIBETON FELL

Bash Mill

Greenwood Hall

Gale Garth

Cragg Hill

Cragg

Banks

Mire House

Dance Croft

Hazel Hall

Lunds Hill

Abbot

Helm Side

Low Barn

Hole Ho

Hawk Raw

Barth Bridge

Wood Head

Mathers

Bons Bank

Row

Bank

Biggerswic

High & Low Halls

Hugh Croft

Kias Croft

HOLME FELL

Bower Bank

Undr Wood

Food Syke

Colm Scar

Low Mill

High Mill Beck

DENT

West Bank

East Bank

Alice Gill

Green Noo

Helks

Coventry

Slack

Noon

Bu

Holl

Extract from map by Thomas Jefferys c.1751